Wildflowers of Cape Cod

WILDFLOWERS of CAPE COD

by

HAROLD R. HINDS &
WILFRED A. HATHAWAY

Photographs by the Authors

Pen and Ink Drawings by
WILFRED A. HATHAWAY

THE CHATHAM PRESS, INC., CHATHAM, MASS.

ACKNOWLEDGMENTS

Many have been of assistance in the inspiration and preparation of this volume, not the least of whom are those questioning people who have asked the naturalists of the National Seashore, "Where can we find a guide to help us with the flowers in this area?"

Sincere acknowledgement is extended to the Department of the Interior personnel of the Cape Cod National Seashore, especially to the first Chief Naturalist of the park, Vernon S. (Tommy) Gilbert, who made the initial suggestion for the writing of such a guide; to his successor, Earl Estes, who laid the groundwork for its publication; and to the present Chief Naturalist, Vernon D. Dame, who helped it to fruition.

We would like to thank Robert Taylor, Clark L. Thayer, John Burk and Robert Boles for their expert advice.

We are indebted to our wives, Judy Hinds and Marion Hathaway, for their cooperation and forbearance throughout the vicissitudes that occurred during the preparation of the material for this book.

Harold R. Hinds
Wilfred A. Hathaway
January, 1968

INTRODUCTION

Today, with automobiles to transport us from one location to another, wildflowers tend to become a blur of colors as we rush past fields and roadsides. We take them for granted as simply being there. Yet, these flowers, which are only one element in the make-up and life of a plant, can become a fascinating and relaxing hobby. It is a pursuit that can lead (on bright days) to remote and beautiful parts of the woods, fields or dunes in search of new specimens; while in poor weather, you can relax with a flower book or magazine, seeking more knowledge of plants you have found or descriptions of those you will seek on your next walk.

In order to separate one type of flower from all others or recognize another of the same kind, it is important to have a name for the plant. Thus, the first purpose of this, as well as most other field guides, is to enable you to answer the question, "What is it?" Secondly, and almost equally important, is the relationship your specimen bears to others of its species and habitat. As you progress in your study of wildflowers, the plants around you will fall into well-organized patterns, each having its own special characteristics within an orderly system.

Over 600 plant specimens have been recorded on Cape Cod. Two-thirds of these, however, are found only in isolated areas, or widely scattered among the common plants. The other third, or some 200 species, are common not only to the Cape, but for the most part to the coastal plains of New England. It is with these species that *Wildflowers of Cape Cod* is principally concerned.

Plants included in this book have been listed in four ways: by keys; by plant descriptions; visually by drawings and color photos; and alphabetically in the index. Since the majority of plants is confined to certain areas where conditions are suited to their particular growing requirements, we have grouped them according to the place, or *habitat*, where they are most commonly found. The boundaries of these habitats merge into one another, and some plants have adapted themselves to two or more habitats. For that reason, you will find a few plants keyed in more than one chapter.

IDENTIFYING YOUR PLANT

If you are using a flower guide for the first time, you will undoubtedly take a quick glance at the keys and decide that they are not for the amateur. On the contrary, while keys may appear complicated at first, they are fun to use, and can be easily mastered with a little practice and patience.

The first step to identification by keys is an understanding of the terms used to describe plants. Imagine that you have discovered some unknown wild plant, and are observing it in its native habitat.

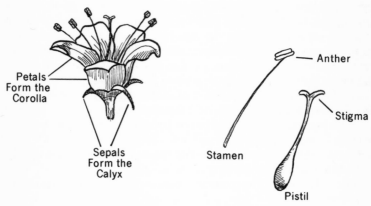

PARTS OF A FLOWER

Perhaps, first of all, you will notice its flowers. Look closely at a new flower to decide whether it is a single flower with numerous parts, or whether it is composed of many, tiny, individual flowers. Diagram 1 shows the principal parts — petals, sepals, stamens and pistils — which together constitute a single *flower*, as in the familiar rose or buttercup. Many blossoms that at first appear to be a single flower are members of the *Composite* family which have many, tiny flowers. Each tiny flower is composed of the principal parts mentioned above, and are massed into a *head*. Plants of this large family on Cape Cod include, among others, the aster, goldenrod, daisy, dandelion, sunflower and black-eyed Susan.

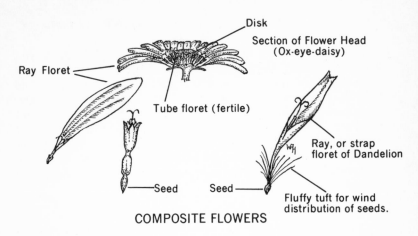

COMPOSITE FLOWERS

There are three general types of composites. First, in the daisy, (Plate IV, No. 5) you can observe many tiny flowers packed closely together in one head. Also in this category are the goldenrod and others which have their tiny flowers grouped into many heads. The outer "petals" of these flowers, called *rays*, are one-sided female flowers, while the inner yellow disk is composed of many, tightly packed, tubular flowers with both male and female parts.

The second and third types of composite are those flowers which have heads composed only of rays or only of disks. One common example of the ray type is the dandelion (Page 59) with its tubular flowers each having a strap-shaped, one-sided extension. The common tansy (Page 53) is typical of the disk type.

Having decided whether your flower is single, or one of the three composite types, you should next consider whether it is *conspicuous* or *inconspicuous*. These terms are fairly obvious, and are used to differentiate plants with easily noticed flowers from those such as grasses, sedges and some oceanside plants whose foliage is more distinctive than their flowers.

Next, observe the form of the leaves. If there are two at each portion on the stem, they are *opposite*. If you see only one leaf at each position, the pattern is called *alternate*. When the arrangement is *whorled*, several leaves surround the stem at each position. Leaves are *compound* when each one is divided into smaller leaves or leaflets. Study the diagrams that follow and compare them to leaves of plants in your yard or nearby fields.

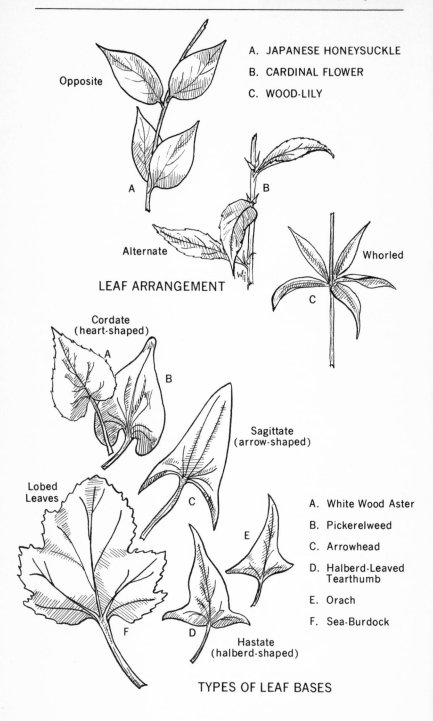

Opposite

A. JAPANESE HONEYSUCKLE

B. CARDINAL FLOWER

C. WOOD-LILY

Alternate

Whorled

LEAF ARRANGEMENT

Cordate
(heart-shaped)

Sagittate
(arrow-shaped)

Lobed
Leaves

A. White Wood Aster

B. Pickerelweed

C. Arrowhead

D. Halberd-Leaved Tearthumb

E. Orach

F. Sea-Burdock

Hastate
(halberd-shaped)

TYPES OF LEAF BASES

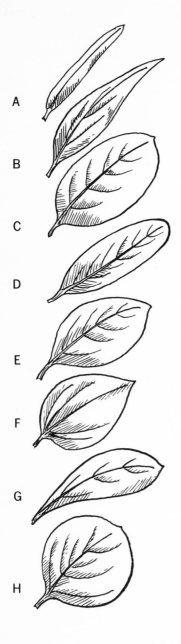

A. Linear
   (narrow)

B. Lanceolate
   (lance-shaped)

C. Elliptical

D. Oblong

E. Oval

F. Ovate

G. Obovate
   (broadest at tip)

H. Orbicular

LEAF SHAPES

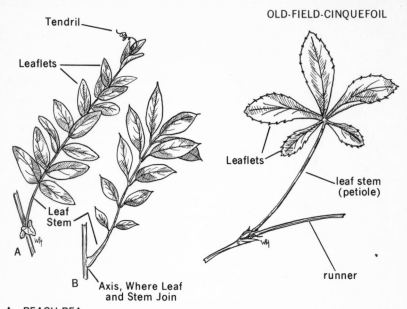

OLD-FIELD-CINQUEFOIL

Tendril

Leaflets

Leaflets

leaf stem
(petiole)

Leaf
Stem

A

B   Axis, Where Leaf
and Stem Join

runner

A. BEACH-PEA

B. POISON SUMAC   PALMATELY
                              COMPOUND LEAF

Botanists distinguish some plants from others by the kind of *fruit* they bear. The term fruit does not necessarily indicate a fleshy growth, but refers to all types of seed containers such as capsules, berries, grains, nutlets, pomes (apple or apple-like fruits), and drupes (cherry-like fruits).

Before identifying some plants with certainty, you will need to examine their stems. The alternatives, *shrubby*, and *not shrubby* or *herbaceous*, serve to distinguish between two fairly obvious categories of plants. A shrubby plant has woody stems and does not die back to the ground each winter. Because these plants also live for more than three years, they are called *perennials*. On the other hand, an herbaceous plant or herb has no woody stem. It may live for one growing season (an *annual*); for two (a *biennial*); or it may be a perennial. *Herbaceous perennials* die back to the ground each winter, but underground stems remain alive in several forms: buds on the top of a root crown, bulbs, corms, or tubers. A *succulent* plant is one in which the stem and/or leaves are thick, fleshy and watery. Many of the seashore and salt marsh plants have this characteristic.

HOW TO USE THE KEYS

Once you have mastered the basic terms, you are ready to follow a key to its destination — the identification of your particular plant.

The secret to keys is the ability to differentiate between the observed features of your specimen and the *opposite* of those features.

The simplest example is found in the Key to Habitats following this Introduction. In this key, the first letter A indicates Uplands; the second A several lines down is Low-lands. You must be in one or the other place; it is impossible to be in both places at one time. Thus, you make your choice between the first and second A. If you are in Uplands, move to the next letter B. The area around you is either wooded or open. If it is wooded, you have reached your goal — Chapter One. If it is open, you still have two choices; recently disturbed areas or areas of low heath. By selecting the proper C, you decide upon Chapter Three or Chapter Two.

The same principal of narrowing your choice by selecting one of two opposites applies in greater depth to the plant keys themselves. By tracing the following example through to its conclusion, you will find how easy it can be to identify plants by keys.

Suppose that you have chosen the Seashore and Salt Marsh Habitat, Chapter Four, from the habitat key. Turning to page 82, you decide first of all that your plant is *not shrubby*. Therefore, you disregard the first a. and all of the entries beneath it, thumbing down until you find the second a. on page 83. You then select the first g., because the flowers are inconspicuous rather than conspicuous; the second h. because the leaves are unlobed rather than lobed.

Making similar choices, you proceed through the second j., the second m., to the first n., which you choose because the stems are lying flat on the sand. At this point, you will make some additional observations. If you notice a sheath at the base of the leaf, encircling the stem, you need go no further in the key; you have identified the plant as the SEABEACH-KNOTWEED, named under the first o. as Figure 83. As a final check, turn to figure 83 and compare your specimen with the drawing and descriptive text.

Always read through both choices to decide which is most appropriate. If your result appears to be in error, check back to be certain you have correctly analyzed the characteristics of the plant, and that you are in the right habitat. Then, work through the key again. After a very few tries you will find yourself running smoothly through them each time.

One final word of caution: before starting on your first self-guided field exploration, learn to recognize three common plants. These are poison ivy and poison sumac (Figure 36), and spotted cowbane (Figure 133). Contact with the first two can cause severe skin irritation; the third is deadly poisonous if chewed or eaten. Recognizing these poisonous plants on sight can save you considerable distress, and will allow you to enjoy all the other *Wildflowers of Cape Cod.*

KEY TO HABITATS AND CHAPTERS

A.   Uplands (areas with relatively dry soil, not influenced by nearness of water). . .B.

   B.   Wooded areas of scrubby or large trees and their dry borders (see Chapter Two for heathland plants straying into open woods):   Chapter One, WOODLANDS

   B.   Open areas. . .C.

      C.   Areas of recent disturbance by man such as roadsides, lawns, waste areas, old house sites, fields overgrown with red cedar, or cleared and scraped areas:
Chapter Three, DISTURBED AREAS

      C.   Areas of low heath or heather-like aspect with close, low-growing shrubs and herbs scattered throughout; low trees common but widely spaced; often extending to sandy borders of woodlands (see Chapter One, above), road embankments and dunes; flowers mostly of spring and summer blooming (see Chapter Six for boggy dune hollows):
Chapter Two, HEATHLANDS AND DUNES

A.   Lowlands (area of open water or moist soil, open or shaded) . . .D.

   D.   Open areas without trees. . .E.

      E.   Areas influenced by the sea and tides, either the sea beach with loose sand, or tidal marshes with richer, darker soil and grassy borders: Chapter Four, SEASHORE AND
SALT MARSHES

E. Areas influenced by fresh water, moist soil, springs, ponds and streams. . .F.

    F. Open bodies of water and the **immediate** shore (see Chapter Four for salt pond vegetation):
                                    Chapter Five, POND AREAS

    F. Moist or wet lowlands often surrounding open bodies of water. . .G.

        G. Lowland areas of present or former cranberry cultivation; moist, sandy, between-dune areas; or quaking, mossy or low shrubby areas or borders of muddy ponds with little or no drainage; flowers mostly of spring and early summer: Chapter Six, BOGLANDS

        G. Open bushy (not tall shrubby) or grassy lowlands often bordering streams; flowers mostly of summer and fall: Chapter Seven, FRESH MARSHES AND MEADOWS

D. Shaded lowland areas with tall shrubs and trees; with or without open water; flowers mostly spring blooming:
                                  Chapter Eight, SWAMPLANDS

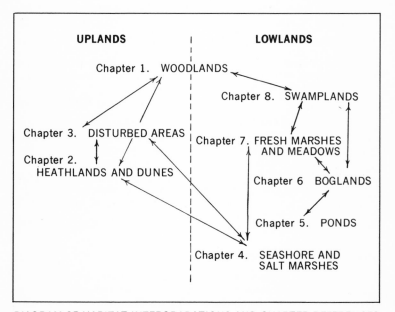

DIAGRAM OF HABITAT INTERGRADATIONS AND CHAPTER REFERENCES

THE MAYFLOWER

In the gleam and gloom of the April weather,
    When the snows have flown in the brooklet's flood,
And the Showers and Sunshine sport together,
    And the proud Bough boasts of the baby Bud;
On the hillside brown, where the dead leaves linger
    In crackling layers, all crimped and curled,
She parts their folds with a timid finger,
    And shyly peeps at the waking world.

The roystering West Wind flies to greet her,
    And bids her haste, with a gleeful shout:
The quickening Saplings bend to meet her,
    And the first green Grass-blades call, "Come out!"
So, venturing forth with a dainty neatness,
    In gown of pink or in white arrayed,
She comes once more in her fresh completeness,
    A modest, fair little Pilgrim Maid.

Her fragrant petals, their beauties showing,
    Creep out to sprinkle the hill and dell,
Like showers of Stars in the shadows glowing,
    Or Snowflakes blossoming where they fell;
And the charmed Wood leaps into joyous blooming,
    As though 't were touched by a Fairy's ring,
And the glad Earth scents, in the rare perfuming,
    The first sweet breath of the new-born Spring.

Joseph C. Lincoln

PLATES

NOTE: Description of the plants included in these plates will be found at the end of the chapters under which they are shown.

WOODLANDS

1. WOODLAND HABITAT

2. INDIAN-PIPE
Monotropa uniflora

3. PINESAP
Monotropa Hypopithys

4. TRAILING ARBUTUS
Epigaea repens

5. SHEEP-LAUREL
Kalmia angustifolia

6. PINK LADY'S-SLIPPER
Cypripedium acaule

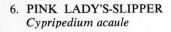

PLATE I

HEATHLAND AND DUNES

1. SEASIDE GOLDENROD
   Solidago sempervirens

2. GOLDEN ASTER
   Chrysopsis falcata

3. HOG-CRANBERRY
   Arctostaphylos Uva-ursi

4. WAVY-LEAVED MILKWEED
   Asclepias amplexicaulis

5. LUPINE
   Lupinus perennis

6. WOOD-LILY
   Lilium philadelphicum

PLATE II

DISTURBED AREAS

1. SCOTCH BROOM
Cytisus scoparius

2. PRICKLY PEAR CACTUS
Opuntia humifusa

3. ORANGE MILKWEED
Asclepias tuberosa

4. CYPRESS SPURGE
Euphorbia Cyparissias

5. CREEPING BUTTERCUP
Ranunculus repens

6. BUTTER-AND-EGGS
Linaria vulgaris

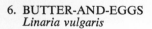

PLATE III

1. **COMMON ST. JOHN'S-WORT**
   Hypericum perforatum

2. **EVENING-PRIMROSE**
   Oenothera biennis

3. **BLACK-EYED SUSAN**
   Rudbeckia hirta

4. **COREOPSIS**
   Coreopsis lanceolata

5. OX-EYE-DAISY
   Chrysanthemum Leucanthemum

6. YUCCA or SILKGRASS
   Yucca filamentosa

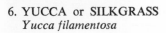

PLATE IV

1. QUEEN ANNE'S-LACE
   Daucus Carota

2. WHITE CAMPION
   Lychnis alba ▶

3. VIRGINIA ROSE
   Rosa virginiana

4. BOUNCING-BET
   Saponaria officinalis ▶

5. COMMON MILKWEED
   Asclepias syriaca

6. CHICORY
   Cichorium Intybus ▶

PLATE V

SEASHORE AND SALT MARSHES

1. SALTMARSH HABITAT

2. SALTSPRAY ROSE
Rosa rugosa

3. BEACH-PLUM
Prunus maritima

4. ROSE-MALLOW
Hibiscus palustris

5. SEABEACH-SANDWORT
Arenaria peploides

6. BEACH-PEA
Lathyrus japonicus

PLATE VI

POND AREAS

1. BUTTONBUSH
Cephalanthus occidentalis

2. WATER-WILLOW
Decodon verticillatus

3. WHITE WATER-LILY
Nymphaea odorata

4. YELLOW POND-LILY
Nuphar variegatum

5. GOLDEN CLUB
Orontium aquaticum

6. PICKERELWEED
Pontederia cordata

PLATE VII

1. SWAMP-MILKWEED
Asclepias incarnata

2. PLYMOUTH GENTIAN
Sabatia Kennedyana

BOGLANDS

3. PITCHER-PLANT
Sarracenia purpurea

4. ARETHUSA
Arethusa bulbosa

5. GRASS-PINK
Calopogon pulchellus

6. WILD IRIS
Iris versicolor

PLATE VIII

FRESH WATER MARSHES AND MEADOWS

1. FRESH WATER MARSH

2. STEEPLE-BUSH
   Spiraea tomentosa

3. COMMON ELDERBERRY
   Sambucus canadensis

4. SHADBUSH or JUNEBERRY
   Amelanchier canadensis

5. RAGGED-FRINGED
   ORCHID
   Habenaria lacera

6. JOE-PYE-WEED
   Eupatorium dubium

PLATE IX

1. **SPIKED LOOSESTRIFE**
   Lythrum Salicaria

2. **GROUNDNUT**
   Apios americana

3. **TURK'S-CAP-LILY**
   Lilium superbum

4. **JEWELWEED**
   Impatiens pallida

5. **SWAMP-CANDLES**
   Lysimachia terrestris

PLATE X

SWAMPLANDS

1. SWEET PEPPERBUSH
   Clethra alnifolia

2. JACK-IN-THE-PULPIT
   Arisaema triphyllum

3. CARDINAL-FLOWER
   Lobelia Cardinalis

PLATE XI

CONTENTS

CHAPTER ONE

WOODLANDS

The best known of the Cape's wildflowers are those of the woodlands. Many, while conspicuous and showy, differ little from the woodland flowers found over much of eastern New England. The porous, sandy soil and salt-laden winds tend to depress the growth of tall trees near the shore, and only in protected areas away from the violent storm winds can they develop. Near the shore, the pitch pine and bear oak occur together in open stands where many of the heath-like plants may be found. The latter plants are found in Chapter Two, Wildflowers of the Heathlands and Dunes.

In the pure pitch pine woods with their thick carpets of pine needles, you may find the spotted wintergreen, prince's pine, maystar, pinesap and shinleaf. Wavy hairgrass is common here also. But where the pitch pine and mature black and white oaks mingle, you will discover the majority of the woodland flowers. Look there for the pink lady's-slipper, Indian-pipe, trailing arbutus, checkerberry and partridge-berry. On the borders of the pure oak woodlands you may come upon the false foxgloves, showy aster, and the bristly sarsaparilla. And in the rare beech tree woodlands, look for the wood aster, beechdrops, wild sarsaparilla and Canada mayflower.

Wildflowers found in wetter, lowland, shrubby or wooded areas are found in Chapter Eight, Wildflowers of the Swamplands.

KEY TO WILD FLOWERS OF THE WOODLANDS

a.   Plants less than one foot tall when flowering. . .b.

   b.   Plants without green leaves, appearing fungus-like but with true flowers, stems, and bract-like, non-green leaves. . .c.

      c.   Plants single-flowered with several stems from the ground, white or pink-tinged, nodding: INDIAN-PIPE (*Monotropa uniflora*)   Plate I, No. 2

   c.   Plants several-flowered, straw-yellow, reddish-orange or purple-brown steaked. . .d.

      d.   Plants occurring near pine trees; entirely straw-yellow or rarely reddish-orange: PINESAP (*Monotropa hypopithys*)   Plate I, No. 3

      d.   Plants occurring near beech trees as a parasite on their roots; stems much branched, purple-brown streaked; flowers small, tubular, inconspicuous: BEECH-DROPS (*Epifagus virginiana*)   Figure 1

 b.   Plants with green leaves. . .e.

   e.   Plants trailing (leaves and flowers very close to the ground). . .f.

      f.   Flowers blooming in early spring, 5-parted, very fragrant, often pink-tinged; fruit a dry capsule: TRAILING ARBUTUS or MAYFLOWER (*Epigaea repens*)   Plate I, No. 4

      f.   Flowers blooming in summer, pure white, fragrant, 4-parted; fruit, a two-eyed, red, tasteless berry; leaves often white lined: PARTRIDGE-BERRY (*Mitchella repens*)   Figure 2

   e.   Plants taller, not trailing. . .g.

      g.   Petals thick, waxy; flowers several on a stalk above the leaves. . .h.

         h.   Leaves rounded, not toothed, shiny green, all from the base; flowers fragrant, nodding: ROUND-LEAVED WINTERGREEN or PYROLA (*Pyrola rotundifolia*)   Figure 3

         h.   Leaves long, narrow and toothed, extending along flower stalk. . .i.

            i.   Leaves dark green with whitish lines down the center: SPOTTED WINTERGREEN or MOTTLED PIPSISSEWA (*Chimaphila maculata*)   Figure 4

            i.   Leaves shiny, light green, not mottled; flowers more numerous: PRINCE'S PINE (*Chimaphila umbellata*)   Figure 4

      g.   Petals not thick and waxy. . .j.

         j.   Petals united to form a tube. . .k.

    k. Flowers not symmetrical, with yellow lower lip; floral bracts deeply lobed; leaves lance-shaped; fruit capsule with wheat-like seeds; low, bushy-branched plant usually found in vicinity of pines: COW-WHEAT (*Melampyrum lineare*)   Figure 5

    k. Flowers symmetrically urn-shaped, extending beneath the leaves; berry fruit cherry-red, wintergreen-flavored: CHECKER-BERRY or TEABERRY (*Gaultheria procumbens*)   Figure 6

  j. Flowers with free petals; spring blooming. . .l.

    l. Flowers very small in a dense, upright cluster; leaves not clustered; fruit a ruby-spotted berry: CANADA MAYFLOWER or WILD LILY-OF-THE-VALLEY (*Maianthemum canadense*)   Figure 7

    l. Flowers star-shaped, 2-4 on thread-thin stalks; several leaves from one spot on stem (whorled); fruit a tiny white capsule: STAR-FLOWER or MAYSTAR (*Trientalis borealis*)   Figure 8

a. Plant about one foot tall or taller when flowering. . .m.

  m. Flowers bell-shaped with flaring lobes. . .n.

    n. Flowers large, yellow, handsome; plants of dry, oak woodlands. . .o.

      o. Leaves finely divided: FERN-LEAVED FALSE FOXGLOVE (*Gerardia pedicularia*)   Figure 9

      o. Leaves broad with pointed lobes: OAK-LEAVED FALSE FOXGLOVE (*Gerardia flava*)   Figure 9

    n. Flowers small, pale green, hanging beneath leafy arching stems: SOLOMON'S-SEAL (*Polygonatum pubescens*)   Figure 10

  m. Flowers apparently not bell-shaped. . .p.

    p. Leaves divided into many leaflets; flowers greenish-white in dome-shaped clusters. . .q.

      q. Stem smooth at base; flowers appearing beneath the leaves; plant of moist woodlands: WILD SARSAPARILLA (*Aralia nudicaulis*)   Figure 11

q. Stem spiny at base; flowers appearing above the leaves; plant of sandy woodlands often extending to roadsides: BRISTLY SARSAPARILLA (*Aralia hispida*) Figure 12

p. Leaves simple (not divided into leaflets). . .r.

r. Flowers in heads with petal-like rays (aster family) . . .s.

s. Flowers white. . .t.

t. Leaves large, heart-shaped at base; flowers in large white-rayed heads; plant of cool, moist woodlands: WHITE WOOD ASTER (*Aster divaricatus*) Figure 13

t. Leaves long and narrow, pointed; tiny flower heads clustered along upper part of stem; plant of dry, open soil or thin woods: SILVER-ROD (*Solidago bicolor*) Figure 14

s. Flowers in large, blue-violet-rayed heads; plants usually massed in dry, open woods and their borders: SHOWY ASTER (*Aster spectabilis*) Figure 15

r. Flowers not in heads; pink petaled. . .u.

u. Plant low shrubby with crowded, light green, round-tipped elongate leaves; flowers clustered; petals united in an open, angular cup: SHEEP-LAUREL or LAMBKILL (*Kalmia angustifolia*) Plate I, No. 5

u. Plant not shrubby; flowers occurring singly at top of stalk; lower petal modified into a large pouch; leaves broadly elongate, rounded, hairy, paired at base of flower stalk: PINK LADY'S-SLIPPER or MOCCASIN-FLOWER (*Cypripedium acaule*) Plate I, No. 6

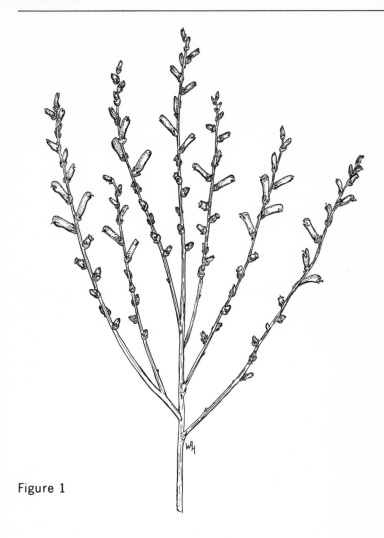

Figure 1

PLANT DESCRIPTIONS

BEECH-DROPS   *Epifagus virginiana*   Figure 1

This slender, branching, purplish or brownish parasitic plant lives under beech trees and absorbs its food from their roots. There are no leaves, only scales along the branches. It cannot be confused with pinesap because of its branching habit. Upper flowers are open, but do not produce seed; the lower flowers are closed and contain the seeds.

PARTRIDGE-BERRY   *Mitchella repens*   Figure 2

This dainty, trailing vine has small, rounded, evergreen
leaves with faintly marked white veins. White or pinkish
flowers bloom in early summer, arranged in pairs at the
tips of slender, leafy stems 2 or 3 inches high. Bright
red berries appear later and remain all winter, unless
eaten by birds.

ROUND-LEAVED WINTERGREEN
or PYROLA   *Pyrola rotundifolia*   Figure 3

The flower stalk rises 8 to 12 inches above a rosette of
thick shining green, rounded leaves which arise directly
from the roots. Flowers have five waxy, rounded petals
and are very fragrant. They grow one above the other
at the top of the flower stalk. The style of the pistil is
noticeably curved and protrudes from the flower. Another
very similar species, SHINLEAF (*Pyrola elliptica*) has
much thinner leaves which are dull and not shining.

SPOTTED WINTERGREEN
or MOTTLED PIPSISSEWA *Chimaphila maculata* Figure 4

This plant is quite similar to its "twin", Prince's Pine,
from which it can be distinguished by its dark green
leaves, strongly marked with white. The edges of the
leaves have only a few teeth.

PRINCE'S PINE   *Chimaphila umbellata*   Figure 4

This attractive evergreen plant grows from 5 to 10
inches high. The stem is leafy, with at least some of the
leaves arranged in whorls. The leaves are shining green
with sharply toothed edges. Very fragrant, nodding
white or pinkish flowers with five rounded petals are in
a cluster at the top of a stem arising from the last
whorl of leaves.

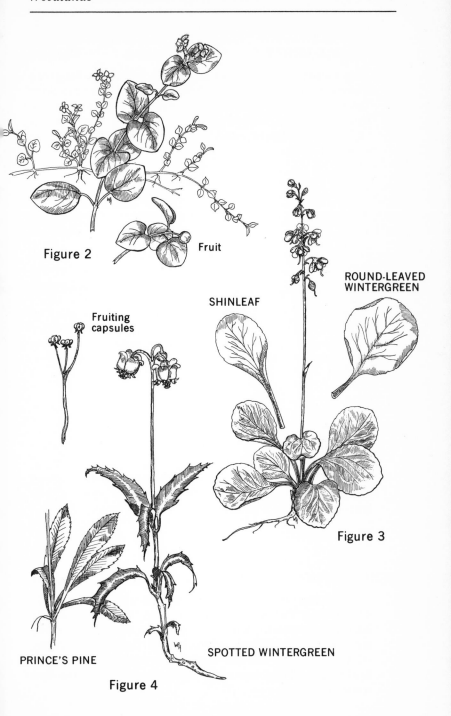

Figure 2

Fruit

Fruiting capsules

SHINLEAF

ROUND-LEAVED WINTERGREEN

Figure 3

PRINCE'S PINE

SPOTTED WINTERGREEN

Figure 4

Figure 5

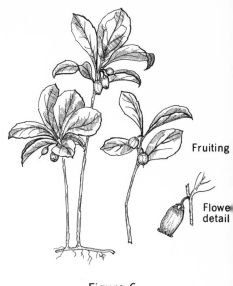

Fruiting

Flower
detail

Figure 6

COW-WHEAT   *Melampyrum lineare*   Figure 5

This erect, low-growing, branching plant would be rather
inconspicuous if it did not grow in masses under pines.
The yellowish-white flowers are found at the point where
leaves and stem join. The flowers have two lips, the
upper arched over the three-lobed lower one.

CHECKERBERRY
or TEABERRY   *Gaultheria procumbens*   Figure 6

The shining, oval, evergreen leaves are all at the top of
this little plant that grows 3 to 6 inches tall. The July
flowers are small, urn-shaped, and hang down from under the leaves. Bright red berries appear later and are
edible. Both leaves and berries have the flavor of wintergreen, another name by which the plant is sometimes
known.

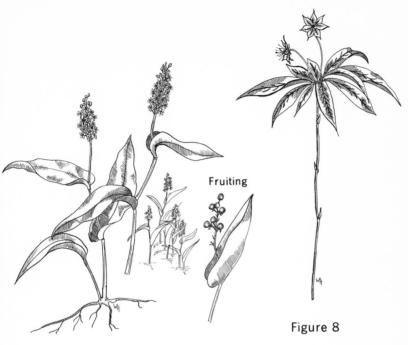

Fruiting

Figure 8

Figure 7

CANADA MAYFLOWER
or WILD LILY-OF-THE-VALLEY *Maianthemum canadense*
Figure 7

This plant is 3 to 6 inches tall and often grows in masses that cover the ground with shining leaves, heart-shaped at the base. A spike of fine, white flowers is borne erect on the single stem, followed by a cluster of red berries. This plant often grows with spotted winter-green, pipsissewa, and pink lady's-slipper.

STAR-FLOWER
or MAYSTAR *Trientalis borealis* Figure 8

The leaves of this plant all grow from one place at the top of a 5 to 8 inch stem. One to four flowers, white and star-like, bloom at the top of a slender, thread-like stalk above the leaves. Star-flowers bloom in late May, frequently with the Canada mayflower.

FERN-LEAVED
FALSE FOXGLOVE

OAK-LEAVED
FALSE FOXGLOVE

Figure 9

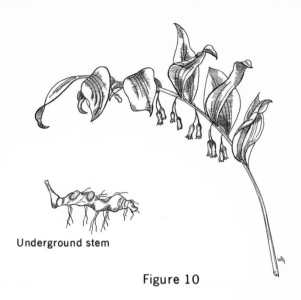

Underground stem

Figure 10

FERN-LEAVED FALSE FOXGLOVE   *Gerardia pedicularia*
Figure 9

Bushy plants, one to two feet tall, bearing large, bright yellow, bell-shaped blossoms with five flaring lobes. The leaves are finely cut and fern-like. This plant blooms in late summer, about the time of the earliest goldenrods.

OAK-LEAVED FALSE FOXGLOVE   *Gerardia flava*
Figure 9

This species of false foxglove is very similar to the preceding, although somewhat taller, often reaching a height of 3 feet. The flowers, too, are similar, but the leaves are broader and the lower ones, especially, are cut into pointed lobes, somewhat resembling an oak leaf.

SOLOMON'S-SEAL   *Polygonatum pubescens*   Figure 10

The leaves of this plant project out from either side of the upper part of the arching stem with small, greenish-yellow, bell-shaped flowers, usually borne in pairs, hanging down along the stem under the leaves. The plant is 12 to 18 inches tall and blooms in late May, about the time of the pink lady's-slipper and the Canada may-flower.

Figure 11

WILD SARSAPARILLA   *Aralia nudicaulis*   Figure 11

The large, divided leaves are at the top of a long,
smooth stalk about 12 to 15 inches tall. The dome-
shaped, greenish white flower clusters are at the top of
a separate stem, shorter than the leaf stem, giving the
appearance of being sheltered by the umbrella-like leaves.

BRISTLY SARSAPARILLA   *Aralia hispida*   Figure 12

This bushy plant, up to 3 feet tall, grows in sandy
places, often along roadsides or edges of woodlands bordering them. In this species of sarsaparilla the greenish
white flowers are in rounded clusters on the same stalk
as the finely divided leaves. After the late June to July
flowers, the bunches of dark blue, berry-like fruit are
more noticeable than were the blossoms.

Detail
near ground

Figure 12

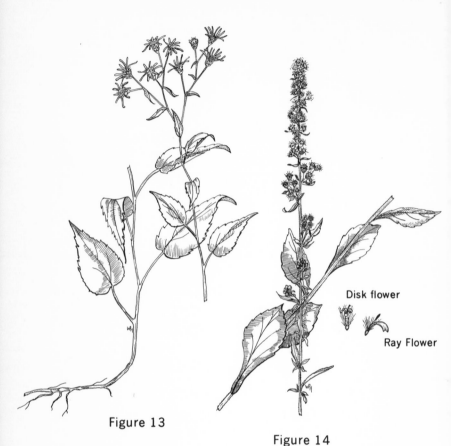

Disk flower

Ray Flower

Figure 13

Figure 14

WHITE WOOD ASTER   *Aster divaricatus*   Figure 13

The large leaves with heart-shaped bases and the clusters of white flowers at the top of a plant 15 to 24
inches tall characterize this aster. It is one of the family
of composites with a yellowish center surrounded by ray-
like "petals".

SILVERROD   *Solidago bicolor*   Figure 14

This slender, wand-like plant, from 12 to 18 inches tall,
is the only goldenrod with whitish flower heads. The
flowers are not numerous and bloom along the upper
third of the stem. The pointed leaves are long and
narrow.

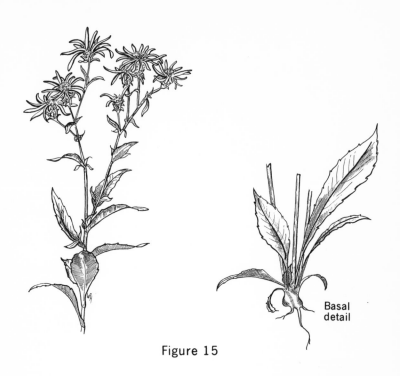

Figure 15

SHOWY ASTER   *Aster spectabilis*   Figure 15

This is the handsomest of the asters with flowers an inch in diameter, deep blue-violet, with a bright yellow center. They bloom in late August and early September, frequently in masses along the roadsides bordering the pine woods.

PLATES

INDIAN-PIPE   *Monotropa uniflora*   Plate I, No. 2

The common names for this summer blooming plant, Indian-pipe, or ghost flower, are appropriate. It is waxy white and "ghost-like", with nodding flowers, borne singly on a stalk, that give it the general appearance of an Indian peace-pipe. It is a parasite, drawing its food from decaying organic matter. It grows from 4 to 8 inches tall, and is found in pine-oak woods.

PINESAP   *Monotropa hypopithys*   Plate I, No. 3

Like the Indian-pipe, this plant is a parasite found in the
same locations and blooms at the same time. It is 4 to
10 inches tall, tawny yellow, occasionally bright red.
When young, the flowers, borne on a single stalk, hang
down like Indian-pipe, but with maturity they stand
erect.

TRAILING ARBUTUS
or MAYFLOWER   *Epigaea repens*   Plate I, No. 4

If any Cape flower deserves special tribute it is the
trailing arbutus. Joseph Lincoln described it beautifully
in his poem "Mayflower" reprinted in the front of this
book. It is an early bloomer, most welcome after the
winter's cold and snow. This trailing plant, with evergreen leaves, frequents the pine-oak woods partly concealed under dead leaves. It has fragrant white or pinkish star-like flowers with a tube beneath the five lobes
of the corolla. Trailing arbutus frequently appears with
checkerberry. When not flowering, it can be distinguished
by its trailing habit and broader, more oval, leaves.

SHEEP-LAUREL
or LAMBKILL   *Kalmia angustifolia*   Plate I, No. 5

This low shrub, from 1 to 2 feet tall, usually grows in
masses. The evergreen leaves are flat and thin, nearly
oblong in shape. A second, light green growth of leaves
frequently appears above the deep pink, flat, cup-shaped
blossoms which are borne in clusters near the top of the
branches. The brown, dry capsules from previous year's
flowers are often present.

PINK LADY'S-SLIPPER
or MOCCASIN-FLOWER *Cypripedium acaule* Plate I, No. 6

The name moccasin-flower is particularly appropriate for
this slipper-like, pouched blossom carried singly on a
waving stalk above two deep green, downy leaves growing close to the ground. The color of the flowers varies
from pale to deep pink; a white-flowered form is rarely
found. It is an orchid and should not be picked.

CHAPTER TWO

HEATHLANDS AND DUNES

The open, rolling, windswept areas of the Cape provide a suitable habitat for many wildflowers. The heathlands or heaths are more or less continuously covered with the ground-hugging bearberry, the lowbush blueberry and black huckleberry, all members of the Heath family. Since the dune areas often have plants in common with the heathlands and usually become stabilized by heathland plants, they are keyed and described below. The open, sandy stretches along the tops of some of the sea cliffs, as well as the dunes of the Province Lands, form a transition between the ocean beach and the woodlands.

Because this habitat is transitional, some plants you find may be listed under open Woodlands (Chapter One), under Disturbed Areas (Chapter Three), or among the Seashore plants (Chapter Four). Refer to these chapters if a specimen cannot be found below.

KEY TO WILDFLOWERS
OF THE HEATHLANDS AND DUNES

a.   Plants shrubby. . .b.

    b.   Leaves fragrant when rubbed. . .c.

        c.   Leaves long, narrow and cut fern-like; fruit a small nut: SWEET-FERN (*Comptonia peregrina*) Figure 16

        c.   Leaves broadly elongate, sparsely toothed, shiny green (substitute for commercial bay); plant bearing in late summer conspicuous clusters of blue-gray, berry-like, waxy nutlets: BAYBERRY (*Myrica pensylvanica*) Figure 17

    b.   Leaves not fragrant; flowers urn or vase-shaped with lobed mouth. . .d.

        d.   Flowers white or pink-tinged, clustered near the tip of foot-high stems; fruit large, blue-coated, sweet: LOW SWEET BLUEBERRY (*Vaccinium angustifolium*) Figure 18

    d.   Flowers reddish-orange, very black, shiny, seedy. BLACK HUCKLEBERRY (*Gaylussacia baccata*)
Figure 18

      e.   Flowers inconspicuous, seen massed in a purplish haze in late April; plant bright green; branches spreading; needle-like leaves tightly enrolled beneath: BROOM CROWBERRY (*Corema Conradii*)
Figure 19

a.   Plants herbaceous, not shrubby. . .f.

  f. Flowers conspicuous and fitting into one of the following categories:
      1.   Flowers with yellow petals or petal-like rays.
      2.   Flowers with white or mostly white petals or petal-like rays.
      3.   Flowers with blue petals or petal-like rays.
      4.   Flowers with red or pink petals.

1. FLOWERS WITH YELLOW PETALS OR PETAL-LIKE RAYS

A.   Flowers in heads (see Introduction). . . . .B.

  B.   Lower leaves darkly purple-veined above; flower stalk about one foot high, branching at the top; flower heads small, rather inconspicuous: RATTLESNAKE-WEED (*Hieracium venosum*)
Figure 20

  B.   Lower leaves not too darkly veined. . . . .C.

    C.   Flower heads densely clustered. . . . .D.

      D.   Leaves large, fleshy; flower heads in large plume-like masses from mid to late autumn: SEASIDE GOLDENROD (*Solidago sempervirens*)
Plate II, No. 1

      D.   Leaves smaller, narrow, aromatic when crushed (anise-scented), flower heads clustered at top of wand-like branches, light yellow in early autumn: SWEET GOLDENROD (*Solidago odora*) Figure 21

    C.   Flower heads larger, daisy-like, in open groups, not densely clustered; leaves long and narrow, covered with long, silvery, silky hairs, low growing: GOLDEN ASTER (*Chrysopsis falcata*) Plate II, No. 2

A.   Flowers not in heads. . . . .E.

E.   Flowers symmetrically 5-parted. . . . .F.

   F.   Flowers tiny, grouped in cushion-like masses; leaves needlelike. . . . .G.

      G.   Flowers with short stalks; leaves spreading from stem, bright green; plant very compact growing: GOLDEN BEACHHEATHER (*Hudsonia ericoides*) Figure 19

      G.   Flowers without stalks; leaves hugging the stem, finely downy or woolly, gray-green; less compact growing: WOOLLY BEACHHEATHER (*Hudsonia tomentosa*) Figure 19

   F.   Flowers larger, not massed, fragile, opening only in sunshine, each for only one day; leaves long oval: FROSTWEED (*Helianthemum canadense*) Figure 22

E.   Flowers not symmetrical, like a small sweet pea; fruit a dark rattle-like pod; leaves 3-parted; two feet high, many-stalked, bushy-branched plant straying from the woodlands: RATTLEBOX or WILD INDIGO (*Baptisia tinctoria*) Figure 23

2. FLOWERS WITH WHITE OR MOSTLY WHITE PETALS OR PETAL-LIKE RAYS

A.   Flowers urn-shaped, pink-tipped; leaves glossy, evergreen; conspicuous plant of open heathland, roadbanks, open pine woods, with scarlet pea-sized berries ripening in late summer: HOG-CRANBERRY or BEARBERRY (*Arctostaphylos Uva-ursi*) Plate II, No. 3

A.   Flowers not urn-shaped. . . . .B

   B.   Flowers conspicuously 5-petaled. . . . .C.

      C.   Plant stem trailing or arching along the ground; stems prickly or bristly; leaves compound; familiar lumpy fruits firmly attached to domed receptacle: BLACKBERRIES and DEWBERRIES (*Rubus* species) Figure 24

      C.   Plant low, but stem not trailing along the ground; leaves 3-divided, each leaflet 3-toothed at summit; fruit a dry capsule: THREE-TOOTHED CINQUE-FOIL (*Potentilla tridentata*) Figure 25

B.   Flowers not conspicuously 5-petaled. . . . .D.

   D.   Plants with leafy stems. . . . .E.

      E.   Clusters flat-topped, of numerous white-rayed heads; leaves broadly elongate, sparsely toothed: WHITE-TOPPED ASTER (*Sericocarpus asteroides*) Figure 26

      E.   Clusters plume-like of small, star-shaped flowers at tip of stem; leaves long-oval, numerous; fruit a ruby-mottled capsule: STARRY FALSE SOLO-MON'S-SEAL (*Smilacina stellata*) Figure 27

   D.   Plant apparently without leaves; flowers small, in wispy clusters, appearing pinkish in fruit; stems appear to be jointed: COAST JOINTWEED (*Polygonella articulata*) Figure 28

3.   FLOWERS WITH BLUE PETALS OR PETAL-LIKE RAYS

A.   Flowers in blue or blue-violet rayed heads. . . . .B.

   B.   Lower leaves with wavy margins and leafy-winged stalks which clasp the stem: WAVY-LEAVED ASTER (*Aster undulatus*) Figure 29

   B.   Lower leaves elongate, round-tipped, with a stem clasping base not contracted: SKYDROP ASTER (*Aster patens*) Figure 30

A.   Flowers not in heads. . . . .D.

   D.   Leaves simple, opposite and wavy-margined; flowers lilac-green in drooping, ball-shaped clusters: WAVY-LEAVED MILKWEED (*Asclepias amplexicaulis*) Plate II, No. 4

   D.   Leaves compound; many leaflets radiating from a central point; flowers sweet pea-like, blue-violet in upright spikes: LUPINE (*Lupinus perennis*) Plate II, No. 5

   C.   Flowers borne singly from the root crown, violet-blue with darker streakings; leaves oval-pointed with several large lobes at base: NORTHERN DOWNY VIO-LET (*Viola fimbriatula*) Figure 31

4. FLOWERS WITH RED OR PINK PETALS

A. Flowers large, orange to orange-red, opening upward; leaves narrowly elongate in several whorls along the stem; fruit a dry capsule: WOOD-LILY (*Lilium philadelphicum*)   Plate II, No. 6

A. Flowers small, pink, orchid-like in a loose, elongate cluster; leaves oval, numerous along the low, weak stems: BITTER POLYGALA (*Polygala polygama*)
                                                        Figure 32

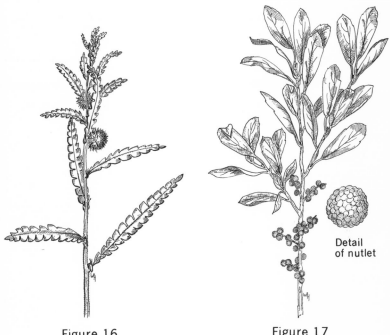

Detail of nutlet

Figure 16   Figure 17

PLANT DESCRIPTIONS

SWEET-FERN   *Comptonia peregrina*   Figure 16

This small shrub grows 1 to 2 feet tall. The narrow leaves are 3 to 5 inches long with deeply notched edges, somewhat resembling a fern leaf. The leaves are fragrant when crushed. Small, bur-like fruits are found in late summer and fall.

BAYBERRY   *Myrica pensylvanica*   Figure 17

Extensive thickets of this compact shrub from 1 to 3 feet high are common. The leaves have several teeth near the tip. The distinguishing mark in the fall is the masses of silver-gray, waxy, berry-like nutlets in crowded clusters along the stem. Both leaves and berries are fragrant. The berries are the source of the wax used in making bayberry candles.

LOW SWEET BLUEBERRY   *Vaccinium angustifolium*
Figure 18

Luscious fruits, varying from cadet blue to purplish black, with a bloom, are borne in clusters on these low shrubs ranging from 8 inches to 1½ feet tall. Shining dark green leaves from ¾ to 1 inch long are narrowly elliptical with very fine teeth. White or pink-tinged urn-shaped flowers with a 5-lobed mouth develop, followed by the berries around mid-August.

BLACK HUCKLEBERRY   *Gaylussacia baccata*   Figure 18

An erect shrub from 1 to 2 feet tall, usually in dense clumps. Its elliptic leaves are green on both sides, toothless, and from 1 to 2 inches long. Flowers grow in one-sided clusters and are urn-shaped, greenish, with distinct reddish-orange marking. The berry is shiny black and sweet, but the seeds are large.

BROOM CROWBERRY   *Corema Conradii*   Figure 19

The spreading branches of this little shrub, from 5 to 12 inches tall, are covered with tiny, bright deep green, needle-like leaves about ¼ inch long. Purplish flowers bloom briefly in late April in tiny clusters at the tips of the branches. Fruit is tiny, brownish black and berry-like, not much larger than the head of a common pin.

GOLDEN BEACHHEATHER *Hudsonia ericoides* Figure 19

This shrubby plant, not over a foot in height, grows in cushion-like masses. Bright 5-parted yellow, star-like, flowers appear in mid-June. The needle-like leaves are bright green, spreading out from the stem on very short stalks.

LOW SWEET BLUEBERRY

BLACK HUCKLEBERRY

Figure 18

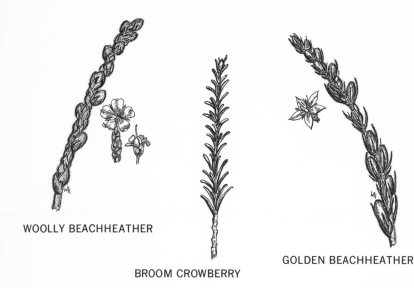

WOOLLY BEACHHEATHER

BROOM CROWBERRY

GOLDEN BEACHHEATHER

Figure 19

WOOLLY BEACHHEATHER *Hudsonia tomentosa*
Figure 19

This plant sometimes called poverty-grass, is similar to the preceding species in its general growth habit and color of flowers. The leaves are very small, gray-green, downy, and pressed closely to the stem. The flowers of both species are on the upper part of the branches.

RATTLESNAKE WEED *Hieracium venosum* Figure 20

The leaves of this plant grow in a flat rosette close to the ground and are marked by purple veins. Flowers are at the ends of slender stalks from 1 to 2 feet tall and look like small dandelions.

SWEET GOLDENROD *Solidago odora* Figure 21

The light yellow blooms of this goldenrod appear in late August and early September. Clumps of 2 to 3 foot-high wand-like stems carry clusters of blossoms at the top. The leaves are narrow and have a faint, sweet odor when crushed.

Mottling
of leaf

Figure 20

Figure 21

FROSTWEED   *Helianthemum canadense*   Figure 22

This dainty little plant of the sandy places grows about 1 foot tall. The flower petals open only once, then fall. The cupshaped blossom is bright yellow and appears in late June and early July. The leaves are small, lance-shaped, with lighter colored undersides and are set close to the stem.

RATTLEBOX
or WILD INDIGO   *Baptisia tinctoria*   Figure 23

This bushy plant is common in dry, sandy areas where it grows 1 to 2½ feet tall. When blooming, it is covered with yellow flowers which resemble a small sweet pea. The leaves are divided into three rounded leaflets and are pale green with a whitish bloom. Flowering time is late July to early August.

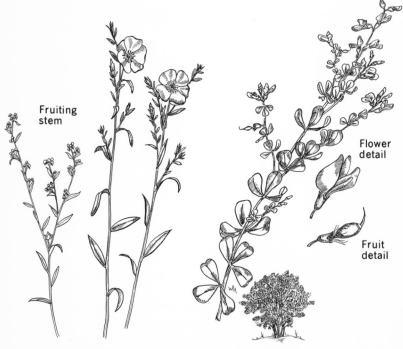

Fruiting stem

Flower detail

Fruit detail

Figure 22   Figure 23

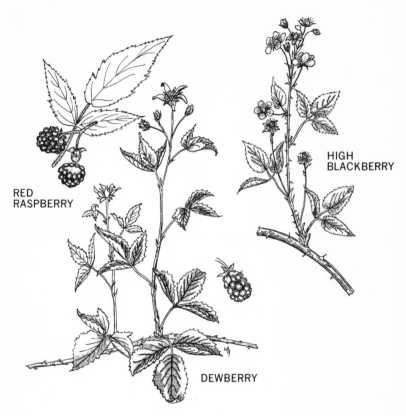

RED
RASPBERRY

HIGH
BLACKBERRY

DEWBERRY

Figure 24

BLACKBERRIES and DEWBERRIES   *Rubus species*
                                                Figure 24

One species of the blackberries is a weak, trailing vine
with reddish stems set with prickles and 3-parted, rarely
5-parted, leaves. Another species is from 3 to 5 feet tall
with stout, arching canes covered with sharp thorns and
thick 3 to 5-parted leaves. The white flowers of both
species are 5-petaled and look like small, single roses.
Fruits are sweet, juicy and edible; they are carried on a
domed receptacle and are shiny black when fully ripe.

THREE-TOOTHED CINQUEFOIL   *Potentilla tridentata*
                                              Figure 25

The low-growing, 4 to 8 inch stems are somewhat woody at the base and arise from a tuft of 3-parted, oblong leaves with three prominent teeth at their tips. The white flowers, in loose clusters, are five-petaled and shaped like a small strawberry blossom. This plant occurs only in scattered locations on the Cape.

WHITE-TOPPED ASTER   *Sericocarpus asteroides*
                                              Figure 26

The slightly angular, stout, somewhat downy, 1 to 2 foot-high stems grow in clumps. The lower leaves start from the perennial root with their toothed blades narrowed and lengthened to resemble a leaf stalk. Progressively smaller leaves extend up the stem to the flat clusters of white flowers. All leaves are faintly three-veined. Blooming time is mid-to-late August with the golden aster.

STARRY FALSE SOLOMON'S-SEAL   *Smilacina stellata*
                                              Figure 27

The erect, or arching, stems of this plant are zigzag, with 7 to 12 alternate, parallel-veined leaves at the angles. The flowers are few and small, white and starlike, borne at the top of the stem. The plants are usually quite numerous in those localities where it is found. Blooming time is late May and early June.

COAST JOINTWEED   *Polygonella articulata*   Figure 28

This plant, seldom over one foot high, arises from a single, rather stiff and wiry stalk with wispy branchlets which appear jointed. The leaves are so inconspicuous that the plant appears leafless. The late September blossoms are pale pink and extend along the branches. When in fruit the plants often give a rosy hue to the areas in which they grow.

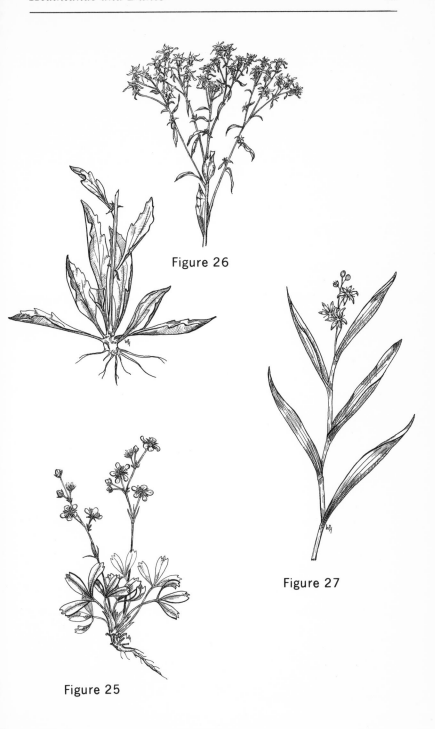

Figure 26

Figure 27

Figure 25

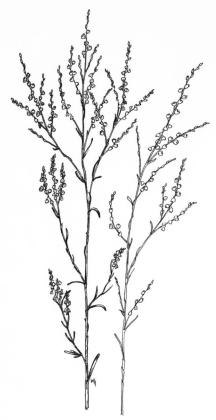

Figure 28

WAVY-LEAVED ASTER   *Aster undulatus*   Figure 29

This 1 to 2½ foot-tall aster is distinguished by its lower leaves. These are rough, with wavy margins, with a base that abruptly contracts into winged stems which dilate and clasp the stalk. The light blue flower heads are numerous and borne on leafy branchlets arising from the main stem.

SKYDROP ASTER   *Aster patens*   Figure 30

The flower heads of this 1 to 2 foot-tall aster are deep blue-purple and showy, and are on widely spreading branches. The oblong leaves, often contracted below the middle, are rough above and on the margins, and have a distinctive base which clasps the stem.

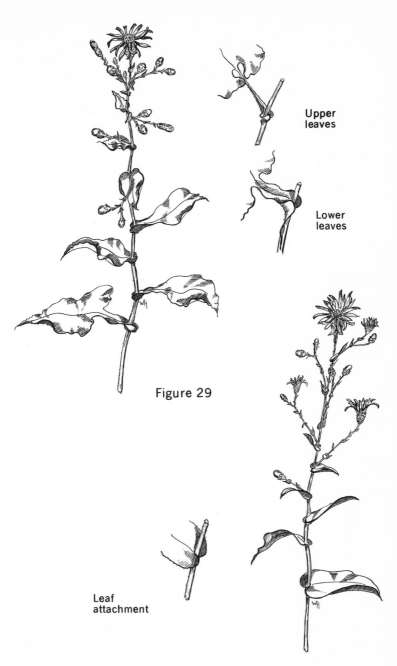

Upper leaves

Lower leaves

Figure 29

Leaf attachment

Figure 30

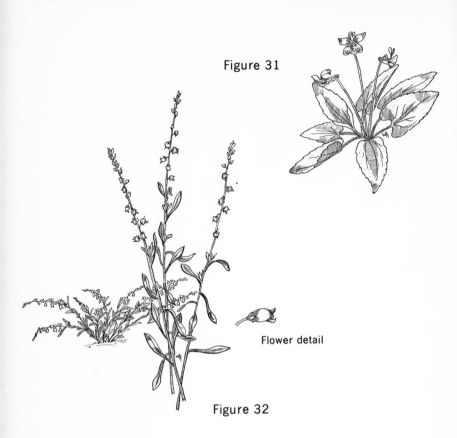

Figure 31

Flower detail

Figure 32

NORTHERN DOWNY VIOLET   *Viola fimbriatula*
                                              Figure 31

The entire plant is downy, sometimes conspicuously so.
The leaves are oval with pointed tips and have several
prominent rounded teeth at the base. The flowers are
violet blue with darker streaks and bloom in mid-May.

BITTER POLYGALA   *Polygala polygama*   Figure 32

Several smooth, erect, leafy stems, simple, rarely forking, arise to a height of 5 to 10 inches. The small,
bright pink flowers are borne at the tip of the stem.
This dainty little plant makes a bright spot of color
among the grasses and lichens of the heathlands.

Figure 33

BEACHGRASS
or MARRAM   *Ammophila breviligulata*   Figure 33

This is the coarse grass, 1½ to 2 feet high, found all
along the sandy beaches. The leaves are long, stiff, with
rather sharp edges, and wave in the slightest breeze.
The flowers are creamy-white in a narrow, elongated,
cylindrical cluster at the top of a stout stem rising
above the leaves in height. The creeping, underground
stems are long, with a very sharp pointed tip. Its strong
root system acts as a deterrent to wind erosion of
dunes and beaches.

Figure 34

WAVY HAIRGRASS   *Deschampsia flexuosa*   Figure 34

This grass grows up to three feet tall with long flowering stalks rising from short, basal leaves. The flower
stalk has many fine, slender branches near the top,
each tipped with inconspicuous flowers. The very slender,
bronzy-purple stalks, swayed by the gentlest breeze, are
often found growing in large numbers, especially on the
sand flats between the great dune ridges of the Province
Lands.

PLATES

SEASIDE GOLDENROD   *Solidago sempervirens*
                                              Plate II, No. 1

The large, showy, clusters of bright yellow flowers grow
in a thick plume at the top of a stout stem 1 to 2 feet
high. The leaves are thick, large, and dark green. This
goldenrod brings masses of color to dunes in September.

GOLDEN ASTER   *Chrysopsis falcata*   Plate II, No. 2

This low-growing plant, scarcely more than 6 to 12 inches high, grows in mats often covering an area of several square feet. The blossoms are bright yellow, in open clusters, and are borne on stems densely covered with furry, grey-green leaves. Golden asters make a colorful display in mid-to-late August.

HOG-CRANBERRY
or BEARBERRY   *Arctostaphylos Uva-ursi*   Plate II, No. 3

This trailing, vine-like shrub hugs the ground with its small, smooth, shiny green leaves crowded along the stem. The white flowers are urn-shaped with pink tips. The bright scarlet berries, ripening in late September, are food for many game birds. This plant makes a thick ground cover in the sandy soil of the open heathlands, as well as beneath the pines.

WAVY-LEAVED MILKWEED   *Asclepias amplexicaulis*
Plate II, No. 4

The stout stems rise 1 to 2½ feet with opposite, pale green, wavy margined, downy leaves. The heart-shaped bases of the leaves clasp the stem. Greenish purple flowers grow in a drooping spherical cluster. The seed pods are 4 to 6 inches long, erect, on recurved stems.

LUPINE   *Lupinus perennis*   Plate II, No. 5

The bright blue-violet, sweet pea-like flowers grow upright in spikes above compound leaves which usually have from 7 to 11 leaflets arising from a common center. This plant frequently grows in clumps of three or four stalks and when in bloom in early June makes a brilliant display. The seed pods resemble small, hard, dark brown peas.

WOOD-LILY   *Lilium philadelphicum*   Plate II, No. 6

This brilliant dark orange-red lily has 1 to 4 open bell-shaped flowers erect on the stem. The leaves are narrow and arranged in 2 to 6 whorls at intervals along the stem. This lily cannot be confused with the Turk's-cap-Lily, which has a large, upright cluster of drooping flowers with recurved, claw-like petals.

CHAPTER THREE

DISTURBED AREAS

On former house sites, in abandoned fields and along the roadside, altogether the largest wildflower habitat, you will find the greatest number of conspicuous "wild" flowers. Most of these plants are not native to the Cape, but were either carried accidentally as seeds in ballast or wool waste, or brought purposely by seamen and settlers who planted them in their gardens for decoration or as herbs for medicines and soothing teas. Since colonial times, these plants have escaped and spread widely throughout the country.

Colonies of the underground spreading, pink-flowered bouncing-bet, the strongly-scented tansy, and the fragrant spearmint often indicate the site of a former house. The colonists used these three plants to color their gardens just as commonly as present generations choose the marigold, petunia and chrysanthemum.

Fields of onions, potatoes, turnips, beets, asparagus and several cereal grasses once covered the Cape, attesting that agriculture, along with dairying, was a principal use of the land several decades ago. Today, however, agriculture clearly plays a secondary role, for the once-open fields have been taken over by many previously foreign as well as native plants. As these fields slowly revert to woodland, the shapely, pointed red cedar first invades them, followed by the straggly pitch pine and black oak. The black and white oak blend with the scattered pitch pines, while in the lower-lying moist sites beech, red maple and black gum grow up again.

The wildflowers along the mostly weedy roadside reflect the areas through which the road passes. Yet, since most roadsides are kept well-mown, they have commonly a heathland or a meadowland aspect. Chapter Two, Heathlands and Dunes, and Chapter Seven, Fresh Marshes and Meadows, should be consulted for upland or lowland roadsides respectively.

KEY TO WILDFLOWERS OF DISTURBED AREAS

a. Plants with woody, perennial branches; shrubby or vine-like. . . . .b.

  b. Shrubby plants. . . . .c.

    c. Green-stemmed, small leaved, yellow-flowering shrub blooming in early summer; of European origin: SCOTCH BROOM (*Cytisus scoparius*)
                                         Plate III, No. 1

    c. Dark-stemmed, larger, aromatic-leaved plant; flowers inconspicuous (sexes on different bushes); fruit clusters of bluish-green, waxy nutlets most conspicuous when leaves drop in autumn: BAYBERRY *(Myrica pensylvanica)*
                               Chapter 2, Figure 17

  b. Vine-like or rarely shrubby plants with a tendency to climb over other vegetation. . . . .d.

    d. Flowers conspicuous, white, turning yellow with age, fragrant; leaves in opposite pairs along the stem; berries black; introduced from Asia, a weedy vine strangling our native vegetation: JAPANESE HONEYSUCKLE *(Lonicera japonica)*   Figure 35

    d. Flowers inconspicuous, yellow-green in axils of leaves; compound, composed of three, mostly oval-pointed, shiny green leaflets which turn brilliant red or yellow in autumn; fruit dry, whitish nutlets (Do Not Touch!): POISON IVY *(Rhus radicans)*   Figure 36

a. Plants without woody branches. . . . .e.

  e. Leaves or stems more conspicuous than the flowers which are small and difficult to see. . . . .f.

    f. Tall (about 3 feet), green, bushy-stemmed plants with fine wispy branches; leaves reduced to scales; scarlet berries ripe in late summer: GARDEN ASPARAGUS *(Asparagus officinalis)*   Figure 37

    f. Shorter plants (under 2 feet). . . . .g.

      g. Leaves long and narrow, grass-like. . . . .h.

        h. Plants velvety-gray except flowers and fruiting sprays which are pale, pink-purple (poisonous, do not chew!) VELVET-GRASS *(Holcus lanatus)*
                                       Figure 38

    h. Plants finely hairy, but not velvety; leaves 3-ribbed and pointed; flowers dull white in a dense spike at top of grooved stalks: ENGLISH PLANTAIN or RIBGRASS *(Plantago lanceolata)*
Figure 39

    g. Leaves finely divided with long, narrow lobes; flowers in a tall, purple-branched spray with numerous greenish heads: TALL WORMWOOD *(Artemisia caudata)*   Figure 40

e. Flowers or flower heads conspicuous, fitting into one of the categories listed below:

    1. Flowers with orange or yellow petals or petal-like rays.
    2. Flowers with white petals or petal-like rays.
    3. Flowers with red or pinkish (not lilac) petals or clusters.
    4. Flowers with blue, violet or lilac petals or petal-like rays.

1. FLOWERS WITH ORANGE OR YELLOW PETALS OR PETAL-LIKE RAYS

A. Plants without petal-like rays. . . . .B.

  B   Flowers in heads of all disk flowers. . . . .C.

    C. Plant low, with finely divided leaves which suggest odor of pineapple when bruised; flower heads domed, dull yellow; locally escaped from the Pacific States, often found along paths: PINEAPPLEWEED *(Matricaria matricarioides)*   Figure 41

    C. Plant tall (about 2 feet) with very strongly scented, finely divided leaves; flower heads flattened, orange-yellow; frequent near old homesteads: TANSY *(Tanacetum vulgare)*   Figure 42

  B. Flowers not in heads. . . . .E.

    E. Stems flattened, thick, fleshy and armed with spines and nearly invisible, clustered bristles; flowers bright yellow, large, sometimes red-centered; fruit reddish, juicy: PRICKLY PEAR CACTUS *(Opuntia humifusa)*
Plate III, No. 2

    E. Stems neither flattened nor bristly. . . . .F.

      F. Flowers in dense clusters. . . . .G.

G.   Flowers bright orange; leaves narrowly oblong, hairy, opposite; fruit an elongate pod with plumed seeds in late summer: ORANGE MILKWEED or BUTTERFLY-WEED *(Asclepias tuberosa)*
Plate III, No. 3

G.   Flowers small, bright yellow. . . . .H.

H.   Leaves thick and succulent, crowded along the stem; low plant appearing as all flowers when viewed from above; occasionally escaped from gardens along roadsides: STONECROP *(Sedum acre)*
Figure 43

H.   Leaves not succulent; light green, narrow and crowded along the stem; flower bracts bright yellow-green in flattish clusters at top of stem: CYPRESS SPURGE *(Euphorbia Cyparissias)*
Plate III, No. 4

F.   Flowers blooming singly or several at one time in open clusters. . . . .J.

J.   Compound leaves of 3 to several, toothed leaflets radiating from a central point. . . . .K.

K.   Compound leaves of three leaflets (like shamrock) flowers with five, bright yellow, rounded petals; fruit a narrow, pointed capsule, small, softly hairy plants with an acid juice: YELLOW WOOD-SORREL *(Oxalis stricta)*   Figure 44

K.   Compound leaves of usually five leaflets. . . . .L.

L.   Plants with weak stems running along the ground; leaves with long stalks; petals deep yellow. . . . .M.

M.   Flowers quarter-sized; bright shiny yellow; often occurring in great masses: CREEPING BUTTERCUP *(Ranunculus repens)*   Plate III, No. 5

M.   Flowers dime-sized, not shiny-petaled; leaves divided into 5 separate leaflets radiating from a central point: OLD-FIELD CINQUEFOIL *(Potentilla canadensis)*   Figure 45

   L.   Plants larger with upright stems; petals pale
        yellow and notched: SULPHUR CINQUE-
        FOIL *(Potentilla recta)*   Figure 46

J.   Leaves simple, not divided into leaflets, but some-
     times deeply lobed. . . . .N.

   N.   Leaves well developed. . . . .O.

      O.   Leaves velvety, gray-green; flowers 5-
           lobed, yellow, arranged along a tall spike
           (up to 4 feet); conspicuous after flowering
           as a sometimes branched, dark brown
           spike roughened with old seed capsules:
           MULLEIN (*Verbascum Thapsus*)
                                          Figure 47

   O.   Leaves smooth or slightly hairy. . . . .P.

      P.   Flowers two-lipped, with a long nectar
           spur at base; lower lip orange, upper
           yellow; leaves long, narrow and pointed;
           summer   blooming: BUTTER-AND
           EGGS (*Linaria vulgaris*)
                                      Plate III, No. 6

      P.   Flowers symetrically 4-or 5-petaled
           . . . . .Q.

         Q.   Flowers 4-petaled, yellow; bottom
              leaves deeply lobed, upper leaves not
              lobed, elongate and usually toothed.
              Tall, rank, weedy plant closely re-
              lated to the cultivated turnip: BLACK
              MUSTARD *(Brassica nigra)*
                                          Figure 48

         Q.   Flowers 5-petaled. . . . .R.

            R.   Flowers golden yellow; leaves
                 round-tipped with tiny light dots
                 when held towards the sun: COM-
                 MON ST. JOHN'S-WORT *(Hyperi-
                 cum perforatum)*   Plate IV, No. 1

            R.   Flowers light yellow, opening at
                 dusk, closing on bright days before
                 noon; leaves sharply pointed, often
                 reddish tinged: EVENING-PRIM-
                 ROSE *(Oenothera biennis)*
                                      Plate IV, No. 2

N.   Leaves reduced to scales; flowers tiny, golden yellow; dwarf, low, many-branched plant: PINEWEED or ORANGE-GRASS *(Hypericum gentianoides)* Figure 49

A.   Plants with petal-like rays. . . . .S.

S.   Flower heads golden yellow with brown center; plant rough, hairy; leaves broad, toothed, alternate along the stem; originally from western United States: BLACK-EYED SUSAN *(Rudbeckia hirta)*
Plate IV, No. 3

S.   Flower heads entirely yellow. . . . .T.

T.   Flower heads large and separate from each other . . . . .U.

U.   Flower heads dandelion-like but smaller, on tall, slender branched stalks; leaves long hairy, deeply lobed, resting flat on the ground in a rosette: CAT'S-EAR *(Hypochoeris radicata)* Figure 50

U.   Heads daisy-like but all yellow; leaves long and narrow. . . . .V.

V.   Heads dime-size; plant low, bushy-branched with numerous, long, narrow, curved, silver-hairy leaves; stem woolly; rays not lobed at tip: GOLDEN ASTER *(Chrysopsis falcata)*
Plate II, No. 2

V.   Heads much larger; rays bright yellow and lobed at tip: COREOPSIS *(Coreopsis lanceolata)*
Plate IV, No. 4

T.   Flower heads small and clustered (Goldenrods) . . . . .W.

W.   Heads in flat-topped clusters; leaves narrow, grass-like: GRASS-LEAVED GOLDENROD *(Solidago tenuifolia)* Figure 51

X.   Stem upright, purple-tinged; heads orange-yellow in spike-like clusters: PURPLE-STEMMED GOLDENROD *(Solidago puberula)* Figure 52

X.   Stem mostly rising on an angle, with the leaves softly gray-hairy; heads bright pale yellow in one-sided clusters: GRAY GOLDENROD or DYER'S WEED *(Solidago nemoralis)* Figure 53

2. FLOWERS WITH WHITE PETALS OR PETAL-LIKE RAYS

A. Flowers in heads. . . . .B.

  B. Heads with petal-like rays. . . . .C.

    C. Heads large, silver-dollar sized with golden yellow center; leaves long, narrow and deeply lobed along their margins: OX-EYE-DAISY *(Chrysanthemum Leucanthemum)*   Plate IV, No. 5

    C. Heads smaller. . . . .D.

      D. Heads tiny, densely clustered at top of stem . . . . .E.

        E. Clusters in a bottle-brush-like formation; stem gray-hairy; leaves broadly flattened; SILVER-ROD *(Solidago bicolor)*   Chapter 1, Figure 14

        E. Clusters in flat-topped formation; stem often spider-webby; leaves finely divided and aromatic; rays sometimes pink-purple: YARROW *(Achillea Millefolium)*   Figure 54

      D. Heads larger, not densely clustered. . . . .F.

        F. Upright bushy-branched plant covered above with small daisy-like heads; leaves short, narrow and stiff: HEATH ASTER *(Aster ericoides)*   Figure 55

        F. Shorter, occasionally branched plants covered with long woolly hairs; small colonies formed by underground stems; flowers surrounded by white papery scales which remain after the true flowers have withered, giving these plants the names, straw-flowers, and everlasting . . . . .G.

          G. Leaves long and narrow distributed along the stem. . . . .H.

            H. Heads urn-shaped, not widely open at the summit; stem and leaves aromatic: SWEET EVERLASTING *(Gnaphalium obtusifolium)*   Figure 56

      H.   Heads globe-shaped with leaves usually whiter and more woolly than the preceding species: PEARLY EVERLASTING (*Anaphalis margaritacea*)   Figure 56

      G.   Leaves confined to the base, elongate, round-tipped, white woolly, especially beneath; sexes in different colonies: PUSSY'S-TOES (*Antennaria plantaginifolia*)   Figure 57

  B. Heads without petal-like rays; clusters flat-topped; leaves narrow and elongate, in whorls around the stem; several stems from the ground: HYSSOP-LEAVED BONESET *(Eupatorium hyssopifolium)*
                                        Figure 58

A.   Flowers not in heads. . . . .I.

  I.   Leaves very stiff, long and narrow, upright from the base; flowers large, nodding, showy, along a tall, branched stalk; mostly seen along the roadsides and old house sites: YUCCA or SILKGRASS *(Yucca filamentosa)*
                                        Plate IV, No. 6

  I.   Leaves not as above. . . . .J.

    J.   Flowers small, in long drooping or erect rounded clusters. . . . .K.

      K.   Clusters elongate, drooping; leaves large, broad and long, dark green; fruit clusters of juicy, dark purple or black *poisonous* berries; stem often purple; a large, often shrub-sized but fleshy plant which can be eaten in the early shoot stage cooked as asparagus: POKEWEED *(Phytolacca americana)*
                                        Figure 59

    K.   Clusters erect. . . . .L.

      L.   Slender plant without conspicuous leaves; stem with jointed appearance; flowers in wispy white or pink upright, elongate clusters; plant of open, sandy areas: COAST JOINTWEED *(Polygonella articulata)*   Chapter 2, Figure 28

      L.   Larger plants with compound or finely dissected leaves. . . . .M.

M.   Base of stem prickly; leaves compound with broadly flattened leaflets; flower clusters domed; fruit black, juicy, insipid: BRISTLY SARSAPARILLA *(Aralia hispida)*
Chapter 1, Figure 12

M.   Base of stem not prickly; leaves narrowly dissected; seeds flat, fringed, borne in a cup at top of stem (bird's nest of ticks with long eyelashes): QUEEN ANNE'S-LACE or WILD CARROT *(Daucus Carota)*   Plate V, No. 1

J.   Flowers larger, not clustered. . . . .N.

N.   Flowers trumpet-like, pleated, with 5 points, creamy-white or lavender; tall, *very poisonous* plant with oval, prickly fruit: JIMSONWEED or THORN-APPLE *(Datura Stramonium)*
Figure 60

N.   Flowers with petals mostly free to base. . . . .O.

O.   Leaves opposite, oval-oblong, hairy; flowers opening usually at night, fragrant, petals notched at tip: WHITE CAMPION *(Lychnis alba)*   Plate V, No. 2

O.   Leaves alternate or all from the root-crown or runners. . . . .P.

P.   Low, running plant; leaves divided into three nearly equal, toothed leaflets; fruit sweet, juicy: WILD STRAWBERRY *(Fragaria virginiana)*   Figure 61

P.   Bushy, leafy plant with round, black, juicy *poisonous* berries; narrow petals bent backward exposing pointed, orange center: BLACK NIGHTSHADE *(Solanum americanum)*   Figure 62

3.   FLOWERS WITH RED OR PINKISH (NOT LILAC) PETALS

A.   Plant vine-like, climbing over low, shrubby vegetation, often with the Virginia rose; flowers trumpet-like; leaves hairy, oval-pointed with deeply-cut base: WILD MORNING-GLORY or HEDGE-BINDWEED *(Convolvulus sepium)*   Figure 63

A. Plant not vine-like. . . . .B.

  B. Stems upright. . . . .C.

    C. Plants with spiny leaves; flowers in rayless heads surrounded by spiny bracts. . . . .D.

      D. Undersides of leaves white-woolly; plant bushy-branched; flowers very attractive to bees for their copious nectar: FIELD THISTLE *(Cirsium discolor)*   Figure 64

      D. Undersides of leaves smooth or slightly woolly; flower heads often densely clustered, plant originally from Europe: CANADA THISTLE *(Cirsium arvense)*   Figure 64

    C. Leaves not spiny. . . . .E.

      E. Leaves narrow and grass-like in opposite pairs along the stem. . . . .F.

        F. Leaves bluish-green, in tufts; flower with 5 pale pink or white, fringed petals, fragrant: GARDEN-PINK *(Dianthus plumarius)*   Figure 65

        F. Leaves dull green; stem hairy; petals smaller, pink with white dots: DEPTFORD PINK *(Dianthus Armeria)*   Figure 66

      E. Leaves broader. . . . .G.

        G. Leaves compound. . . . .H.

          H. Leaves with three, narrow leaflets; flowers closely grouped in pinkish-gray, soft-hairy clusters: RABBIT-FOOT CLOVER *(Trifolium arvense)*   Figure 67

          H. Leaves of seven-toothed leaflets; flowers large, fragrant, pink, five-petaled with yellow center; fruit (hip) bright red, berry-like; stems thorny: VIRGINIA ROSE *(Rosa virginiana)*
    Plate V, No. 3

        G. Leaves simple, plants over 2 feet tall. . . . .I.

          I. Leaves alternate. . . . .J.

            J. Flowers in an upright spike, pink; fruit an elongate capsule splitting to release tiny seeds with silky parachutes: FIREWEED or GREAT WILLOW-HERB *(Epilobium angustifolium)*   Figure 68

J. Flowers small in dense, elongate, drooping clusters; loosely-branched plants with swollen stem joints; leaves often with dark blotch in middle of upper side: LADY'S-THUMB *(Polygonum Persicaria)* Figure 69

I. Leaves opposite, oval-rounded; flowers pink, 5-petaled in circles around stem tip; common near old house sites: BOUNCING-BET or SOAPWORT *(Saponaria officinalis)*
Plate V, No. 4

B. Stem reclining, branching close to the ground. . . . .K.

K. Leaves finely dissected; flowers 5-petaled, rose-pink to purple; fruit capsule long and pointed: STORKS-BILL *(Erodium cicutarium)* Figure 70

K. Leaves not dissected, flowers 5-petaled. . . . .L.

L. Delicate, tiny-leaved, weak-stemmed plant with paired, triangular, papery bracts at base of leaves: PINK SAND-SPURREY *(Spergularia rubra)*
Figure 71

L. Larger, oval-leaved plant with orange-red flowers which quickly close in cloudy weather, opening again in sunlight: SCARLET PIMPERNEL or POORMAN'S WEATHERGLASS *(Anagallis arvensis)* Figure 72

4. FLOWERS WITH BLUE, VIOLET OR LILAC PETALS OR PETAL-LIKE RAYS

A. Plant weak-stemmed, vine-like; leaves often deeply lobed at base; flowers orange-centered with purple petals bent backwards; fruit bright red, clustered, juicy but *poisonous:* BITTERSWEET NIGHTSHADE *(Solanum dulcamara)* Figure 62

A. Plants not vine-like. . . . .B.

B. Tall plants (more than 2 feet tall). . . . .C.

C. Flowers small, in clusters, with stalks all from one point, leaves opposite, broad, thickish; fruit a large pod with plumed seeds. . . . .D.

D. Leaves wavy-margined; flowers pale lilac-green: WAVY-LEAVED MILKWEED *(Asclepias amplexicaulis)* Chapter 2, Plate II, No. 4

D. Leaves more flattened, hairy beneath; flowers dull purple: COMMON MILKWEED *(Asclepias syriaca)* · Plate V, No. 5

C. Flowers in pure, light blue, half-dollar-sized heads, soon closing in bright sun; tall flower stalks with small tufts of leaves: CHICORY (*Cichorium Intybus*) Plate V, No. 6

B. Shorter plants. . . . .E.

E. Flowers with an upper and lower lip, not in heads . . . . .F.

F. Leaves and flowers directly from a root-crown; leaves triangular-shaped with lobed base; flowers violet-purple or rarely white: NORTHERN DOWNY VIOLET (*Viola fimbriatula*) Chapter 2, Figure 31

F. Leaves and flowers borne along an upright stem . . . . .G.

G. Flowers very small, light blue, near top of nearly leafless stalk; leaves small, inconspicuous, mostly at the base: OLD-FIELD-TOAD-FLAX (*Linaria canadensis*) Figure 73

G. Flowers larger, dark blue with yellow pollen-bearing parts curled down from top; stem square, hairy; leaves opposite: BLUECURLS (*Trichostema dichotomum*) Figure 74

E. Flowers in heads; often growing on roadsides . . . . .H.

H. Leaves short and narrow, stiff and rough-margined; rays blue-violet to white; plant growing in tussocks: STIFF-LEAVED ASTER (*Aster linariifolius*) Figure 75

H. Leaves narrowly oblong to rounded, pointed; rays bright violet-purple, in loose colonies: SHOWY ASTER (*Aster spectabilis*) Chapter 1, Figure 15

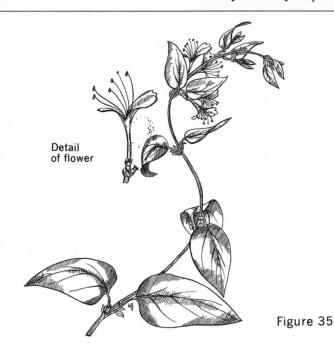

Detail
of flower

Figure 35

PLANT DESCRIPTIONS

JAPANESE HONEYSUCKLE   *Lonicera japonica*   Figure 35.

The fragrant flowers of this climbing vine hardly compensate for its tendency to overrun other vegetation and
form dense thickets. The opposite, narrowly oval, nearly
evergreen leaves have toothless margins. The funnel-
shaped flowers, with five irregular flaring petals, are
white to pinkish, turning yellow with age. The fruit is
a black berry.

POISON IVY   *Rhus radicans*   Figure 36.

This plant, which causes severe skin irritation, climbs
trees, walls and fences by means of rootlets. It is also
found low-growing and erect, spreading over large areas.
The compound leaf has three leaflets, oval with pointed
tips. The small flowers are greenish white and grow in
clusters at the points where leaf stem and plant stalk
meet, followed by small, brownish-white, berry-like
fruits. The non-poisonous Virginia creeper, often mis-
taken for poison ivy, has five leaflets and clusters of
blue-black berries.

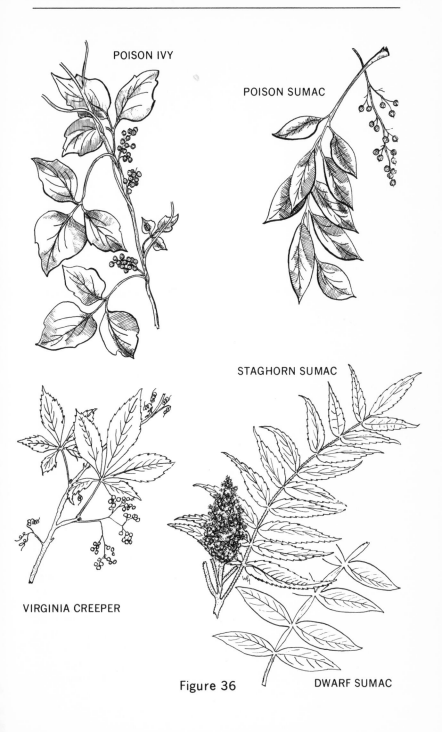

POISON IVY

POISON SUMAC

STAGHORN SUMAC

VIRGINIA CREEPER

Figure 36

DWARF SUMAC

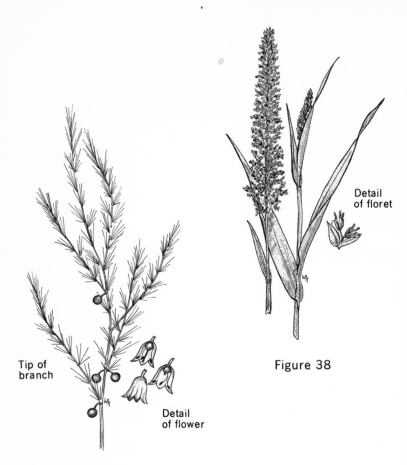

Tip of
branch

Detail
of flower

Figure 37

Detail
of floret

Figure 38

GARDEN ASPARAGUS   *Asparagus officinalis*   Figure 37

This plant, growing about 3 feet high is an escapee from
cultivation. It is of bushy growth habit, light green, with
many fine branches and scale-like leaves. Small, bright
scarlet berries appear in late August.

VELVET-GRASS   *Holcus lanatus*   Figure 38

This conspicuous grass, growing in clumps about 2 feet
high, is grayish and hairy with broad leaf blades. The
flowers, seeds, and the stalks on which they are borne,
are purplish. Poisonous if chewed.

Figure 39

ENGLISH PLANTAIN or RIBGRASS   *Plantago lanceolata*
Figure 39

The leaves arise from a thick root-stalk and grow in a
tight cluster close to the ground. They are hairy, but not
velvety, long and narrow, with three prominent ribs.
The flowers are tiny, white, in a dense conical spike at
the tip of a leafless, erect, ribbed stem. This is a trou-
blesome weed in lawns and grasslands.

TALL WORMWOOD   *Artemisia caudata*   Figure 40

The rosette of very finely divided grey-green leaves grows directly from the root-stalk. Flowers appear the second year and are green to bronze; they are borne on the many erect, tapering, plume-like branches.

PINEAPPLEWEED   *Matricaria matricarioides*   Figure 41

This many-branched plant, 12 to 18 inches tall, has alternate leaves two or three times dissected into short, very narrow, linear lobes. The flowers form yellow domed disks without ray flowers; they are a distinguishing mark of this plant.

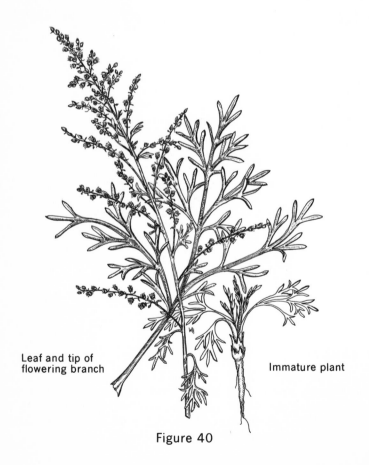

Leaf and tip of
flowering branch   Immature plant

Figure 40

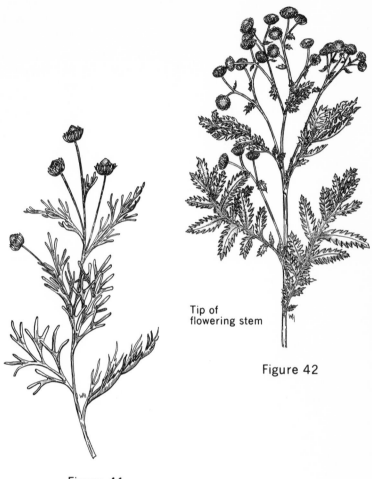

Tip of
flowering stem

Figure 42

Figure 41

TANSY   *Tanacetum vulgare*   Figure 42

The leaves of this aromatic plant are deeply cut into
many fine segments which become progressively smaller
toward the base. The orange-yellow flowers are in flat
clusters at the top of a stiff, erect stem. The plant is
another escapee from herb gardens.

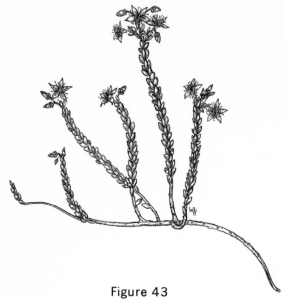

Figure 43

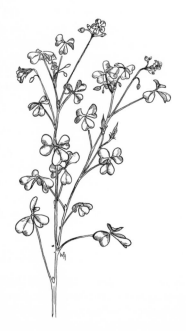

Figure 44

Figure 45

STONECROP   *Sedum acre*   Figure 43

This spreading, matted, moss-like plant has tiny, alternate, fleshy leaves crowded along the 2 to 3 inch-high
stem. The relatively large, star-shaped, 5-petaled flowers
are bright yellow and grow at the tips of the stems. It
is an escapee from gardens, and may be found in abund-
ance along the road cuts on Route 6 between Truro and
Provincetown.

YELLOW WOOD-SORREL   *Oxalis stricta*   Figure 44

The slender, branching stems, rising 4 to 10 inches, have
soft, whitish hairs. The compound leaves, with leaf stems
much longer than the leaves, have three heart-shaped
leaflets and resemble a clover or shamrock. The 5-petaled
flowers are bright yellow. The fruit is a small, pointed,
angled capsule.

OLD-FIELD CINQUEFOIL   *Potentilla canadensis*   Figure 45

This is a frail, vine-like plant with soft, silky hairs on
the stems and lower surfaces of the leaves. The dull
yellow flowers are 5-petaled. Leaves are compound with
five radiating leaflets, the middle one the longest, all
with coarse teeth above the middle.

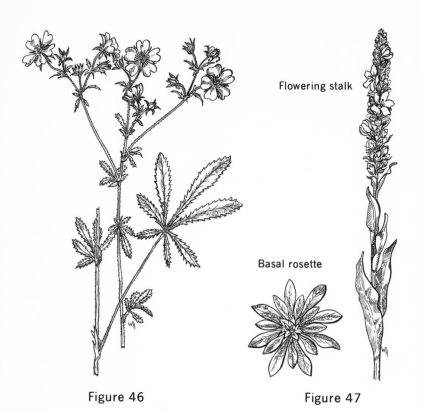

Flowering stalk

Basal rosette

Figure 46   Figure 47

SULPHUR CINQUEFOIL   *Potentilla recta*   Figure 46

The stout, erect stem is 1-2 feet tall, much-branched above. The compound leaves, with 5-7 leaflets, are grey-green above, paler beneath, the lower ones with long leaf stems. Stems and leaves have many soft, fine hairs. The single yellow flowers, up to an inch across, have five heart-shaped petals.

MULLEIN   *Verbascum Thapsus*   Figure 47

The tall, stout, woody stem, 3 to 5 feet tall, growing from a large rosette of velvety, grey-green leaves will identify this plant. The dense spike of yellow, 5-lobed flowers blooms along the upper third of the stem. Dry, brown stalks with many old seed capsules persist all winter.

BLACK MUSTARD   *Brassica nigra*   Figure 48

This tall, rank growing, much-branched plant is 1 to 2½ feet tall. It is somewhat hairy. The leaves are bright green, the lower ones with a slender stem and lobed; those on the main stem are not lobed. The small, four-petaled flowers are yellow and grow in loose clusters at the ends of the branches.

PINEWEED
or ORANGE-GRASS   *Hypericum gentianoides*   Figure 49

The awl-shaped, scale-like, minute leaves are pressed against wiry stems. The plant has erect branches close together. The flowers are very small, 5-petaled, and golden yellow.

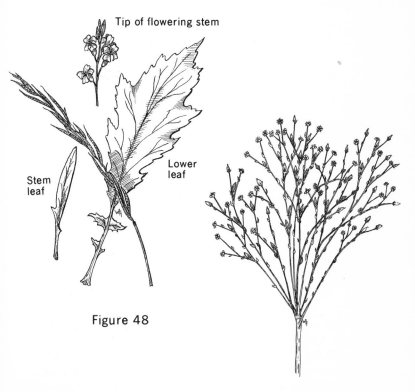

Tip of flowering stem

Lower leaf

Stem leaf

Figure 48

Figure 49

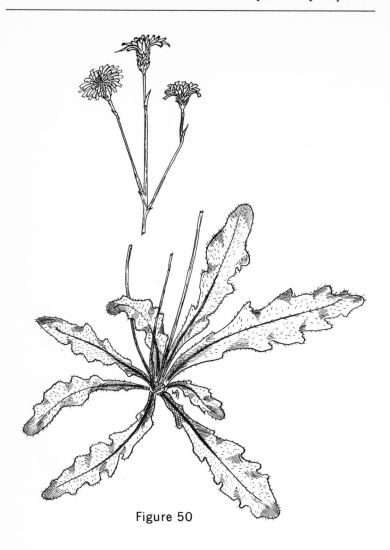

Figure 50

CAT'S-EAR   *Hypochoeris radicata*   Figure 50

The long, hairy, deeply cut leaves of this plant grow in
a rosette close to the ground. From this leaf cluster
arise slender, branched flower stalks bearing yellow
flower heads resembling small dandelions. Abandoned
fields are sometimes covered with the flowers of this
plant from late June to mid-July, blooming along with
the daisies and purple vetch.

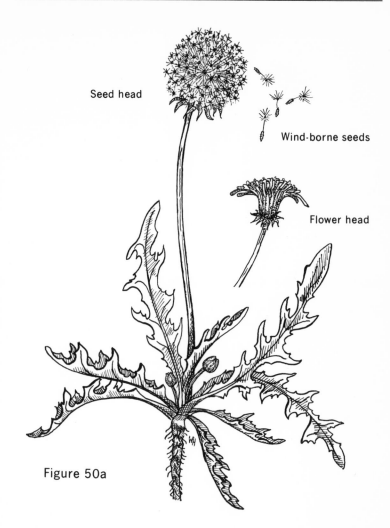

Seed head

Wind-borne seeds

Flower head

Figure 50a

DANDELION   *Taraxacum officinale*   Figure 50a

The rosette of jagged edged, deeply-lobed and toothed leaves grow close to the ground and arise from a long, stout tap-root. The bright yellow flower heads, up to 2 inches in diameter, are borne singly at the top of hollow stems. Flowers are followed by downy seed balls carrying many silk-tufted seeds which are carried away by the wind. This method of seed distribution accounts for the widespread occurrence of this plant, whose gay blossoms compensate for its weed-like tendencies.

Tip of
flowering stem

Figure 51

GRASS-LEAVED GOLDENROD   *Solidago tenuifolia*
                                                    Figure 51

The narrow, grass-like leaves have one or two faintly
marked veins. The flower heads are small and in characteristic flat clusters at the tops of the 1 to 1½ foot-
high stalks. This is the usual flat-topped goldenrod found
in our area; another species, *Solidago graminifolia*, is
similar but has 2 to 4 well-marked veins extending the
length of the leaves.

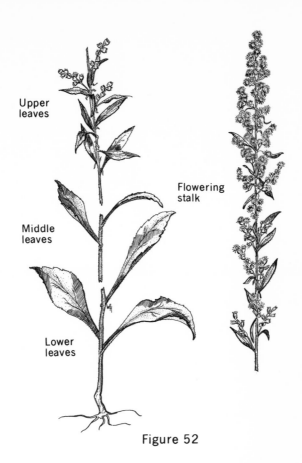

Upper leaves

Flowering stalk

Middle leaves

Lower leaves

Figure 52

PURPLE-STEMMED GOLDENROD   *Solidago puberula*
Figure 52

This 1½ to 2½ foot-high goldenrod, with its purplish stems and bright yellow, bottle-brush-like spike of flower heads is a common sight along roadsides in August.

GRAY GOLDENROD
or DYER'S WEED   *Solidago nemoralis*   Figure 53

This goldenrod usually grows slantwise from a basal rosette of leaves. The entire plant is gray-green and hairy. The flower heads are in plume-like, one-sided clusters, arching over at the tips.

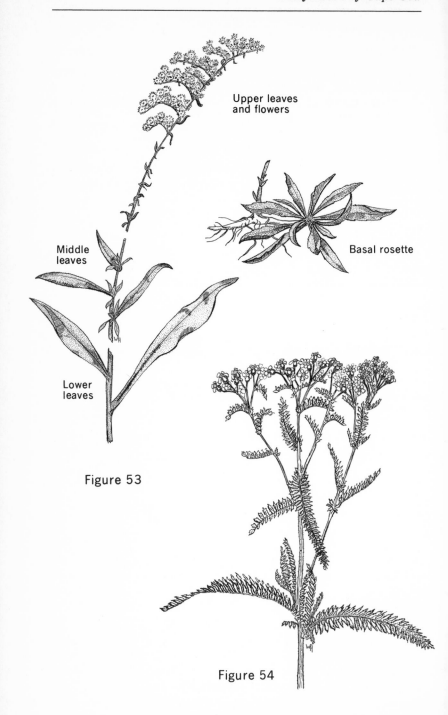

Upper leaves
and flowers

Basal rosette

Middle
leaves

Lower
leaves

Figure 53

Figure 54

YARROW *Achillea Millefolium* Figure 54

The unbranched stem, 1½ to 2 feet high, has many very finely cut, fern-like, strongly-scented leaves, topped by a flat cluster of white flower heads. A rosy-purple form of this plant is sometimes found.

HEATH ASTER *Aster ericoides* Figure 55

This is a wand-like, spreading, branched plant with minute hairs. The very numerous flower heads look like small white daisies.

Detail of branch departure

Figure 55

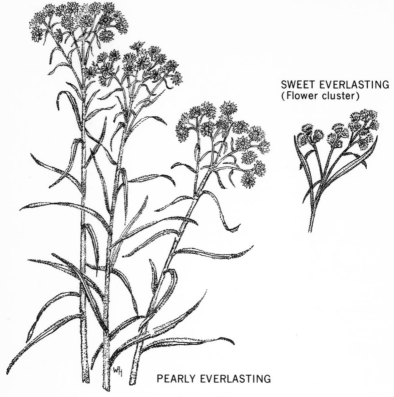

SWEET EVERLASTING
(Flower cluster)

PEARLY EVERLASTING

Figure 56

SWEET EVERLASTING   *Gnaphalium obtusifolium*
Figure 56

This is a gray-green, woolly plant growing in clumps 1 to 1½ feet tall. The flat clusters of urn-shaped flower heads show faintly yellow at the tips and are surrounded by whitish scales. The stems and leaves have a pleasant, aromatic scent. The dried leaves and flowers were sometimes used to make fragrant pillows.

PEARLY EVERLASTING   *Anaphalis margaritacea*
Figure 56

This is very similar to the preceding species, but the leaves are more woolly and much whiter beneath. The flower heads are more globe-shaped than urn-shaped.

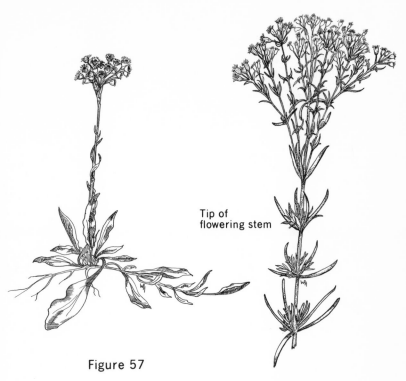

Tip of
flowering stem

Figure 57

Figure 58

PUSSY'S-TOES   *Antennaria plantaginifolia*   Figure 57

This small plant grows only 3 to 9 inches tall. It is a
whitish-grey-green color, silky or woolly all over. The
leaves from the root are oval with three veins; few, if
any, leaves found on the flowering stems are very small
and lance-shaped. Flower heads are yellowish white,
crowded into clusters.

HYSSOP-LEAVED BONESET   *Eupatorium hyssopifolium*
Figure 58

The flowering stems grow in a clump 1 to 2 feet tall.
The long, narrow, grey-green leaves are numerous and
arranged in whorls. Flower clusters are white and flat,
the individual flower heads having petal-like rays.

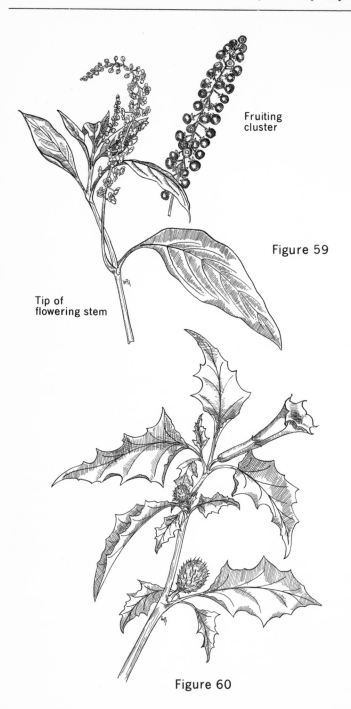

Fruiting
cluster

Figure 59

Tip of
flowering stem

Figure 60

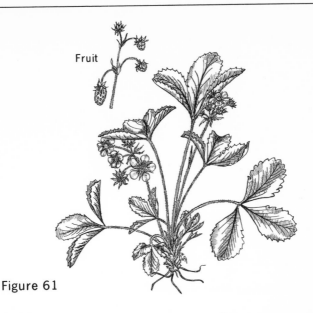

Fruit

Figure 61

POKEWEED　　　　*Phytolacca americana*　　　Figure 59

This bushy plant has heavy, smooth stems, sometimes tinged with reddish-purple, growing to a height of six feet or more. Leaves are large, dark green, broad, and arranged alternately on the stem. The long clusters of small white flowers are followed by dark purple berries. The large, fleshy root and the berries are poisonous.

JIMSONWEED
or THORN-APPLE　　　*Datura Stramonium*　　　Figure 60

This dangerous, poisonous plant grows from 1½ to 2½ feet high with greenish-purple stems. The general outline of the leaves is oval with a pointed tip narrowed at the base to join a long leaf stem. The irregular leaf lobes are also pointed. The large, white, 5-lobed, tubular flower is borne erect on a short stem. The fruit is an oval capsule covered with dense, sharp prickles.

WILD STRAWBERRY　　*Fragaria virginiana*　　　Figure 61

These stemless, rather stout, fuzzy plants have runners that take root along the ground. The 3-parted leaves arise from a tuft just above the root. The white, 5-petaled flowers with yellow stamens are followed by a sweet, juicy, red berry.

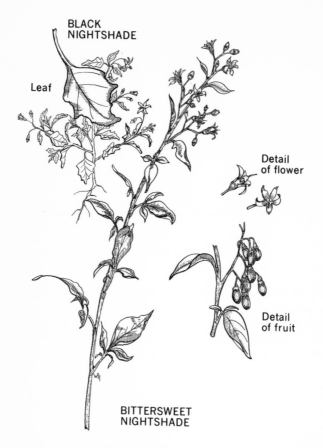

BLACK
NIGHTSHADE

Leaf

Detail
of flower

Detail
of fruit

BITTERSWEET
NIGHTSHADE

Figure 62

BITTERSWEET NIGHTSHADE   *Solanum dulcamara*
                                        Figure 62

The straggling stem of this plant is branched and somewhat woody below. The alternate leaves are very irregular. Some are without lobes, some have one or two
lobes, but all are slightly heart-shaped at the base.
Flowers have orange-yellow centers and five purple
petals which bend backwards. The bright red, oval
berries hang in attractive clusters. The berries are
poisonous.

Figure 63

BLACK NIGHTSHADE   *Solanum americanum*   Figure 62

This erect, much-branched plant grows from 1 to 2½ feet tall. The wavy margined leaves are oval and frequently unequal sided. The flowers are white or faintly purplish. with prominent yellow centers extending beyond the petals. The fruit is a poisonous black berry.

WILD MORNING-GLORY
or HEDGE-BINDWEED   *Convolvulus sepium*   Figure 63

This climbing, twining vine has triangular leaves on slender stems, pointed at the apex and deeply notched at the base. The bell-shaped flowers have slightyl 5-lobed margins and are pink with white stripes or entirely white.

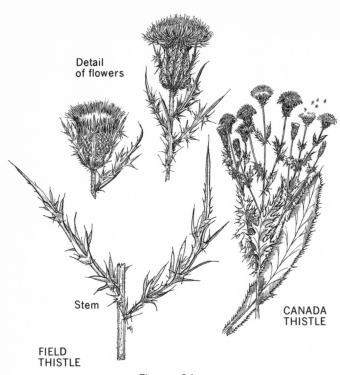

Detail
of flowers

Stem

FIELD
THISTLE

CANADA
THISTLE

Figure 64

FIELD THISTLE   *Cirsium discolor*   Figure 64

Thistles are easily identified by the deeply-notched, oblong leaves armed with an array of stout, very sharp
spines. The brush-like flower heads are rosy purple, followed by seeds with soft, silky, thread-like tufts easily
carried by the wind to considerable distances. This
species has leaves heavily woolly-white beneath and is
not as branched as the Canada thistle.

CANADA THISTLE   *Cirsium arvense*   Figure 64

The spiny leaves of this species are only slightly woolly
on the underside. This thistle often grows to a height of
five feet and is much-branched with light, pinkish purple
flower heads borne singly at the ends of the erect, leafy
stems.

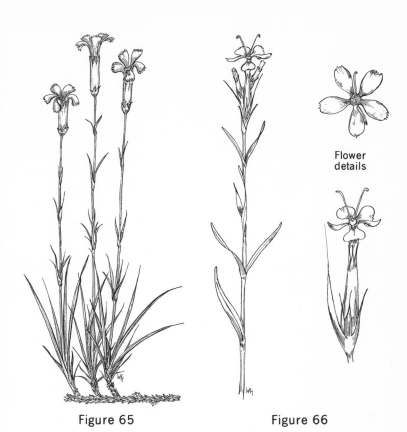

Figure 65   Figure 66

GARDEN-PINK   *Dianthus plumarius*   Figure 65

The stems and narrow, erect leaves, tufted at the base, are a light, bluish-green with a whitish bloom. The flower stems have several pairs of opposite leaves along their length. The flowers are single on the stems with five pink or white heavily fringed petals. The flowers have a clove fragrance. Garden-pink is an escapee from cultivation.

DEPTFORD PINK   *Dianthus Armeria*   Figure 66

This dainty little plant seldom grows over a foot tall. Its narrow, dull green leaves are grass-like. The small flowers, pink with tiny white dots, are in tightly branched clusters at the top of the stiff, softly hairy stem.

RABBIT-FOOT CLOVER   *Trifolium arvense*   Figure 67

This silky, branching, softly hairy plant, 9 to 15 inches tall, has small leaves with three narrow leaflets. The greyish-pink flower heads are furry and arranged in clusters, somewhat resembling a rabbit's foot.

FIREWEED
or GREAT WILLOW-HERB   *Epilobium angustifolium*
                                                Figure 68

A tall plant, often 5 feet high, with very short stemmed, narrowly lance-shaped leaves. The 4-petaled flowers are showy, bright pinkish purple, in slender spikes at the ends of the stems. The seeds, silk-tufted in long, slender brown capsules, are distributed by the wind.

Detail
of capsule
and seed

Figure 67   Figure 68

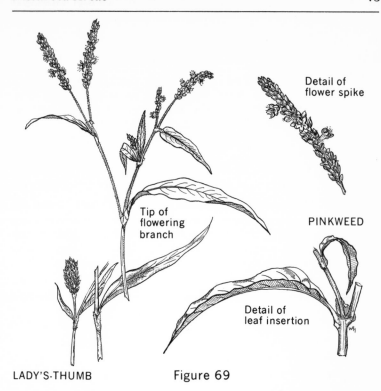

Detail of flower spike

Tip of flowering branch

PINKWEED

Detail of leaf insertion

LADY'S-THUMB   Figure 69

LADY'S-THUMB   *Polygonum Persicaria*   Figure 69

This branching, slender stemmed plant grows up to 2½ feet tall. The narrowed, lance-shaped leaves taper at both ends; they are dotted, frequently with a triangular or half-moon-shaped dark blotch near the center of the upper surface. Dense, cylindrical clusters of pink flowers are at the ends of the branches. Small, light-colored, tissue-thin, tubular structures at the points where leaves and stem meet give the joints a somewhat swollen appearance.

PINKWEED   *Polygonum pensylvanicum*   Figure 69

This pink knotweed often grows to a height of 4 feet in extensive, colorful masses. The large, bright green lance-shaped leaves are larger and somewhat broader at the base than the lady's-thumb (*Polygonum Persicaria*). The flower clusters at the ends of the wand-like branches are longer than the lady's-thumb and inclined to droop.

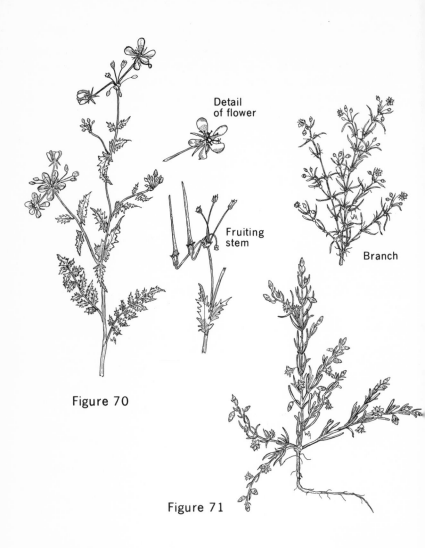

Detail of flower

Fruiting stem

Branch

Figure 70

Figure 71

STORKSBILL   *Erodium cicutarium*   Figure 70

A small, dainty, hairy plant 6 to 12 inches tall with lace-like, very finely divided leaves. The small flowers are purple to pink with five petals and bloom one or two at a time in loose clusters. The seed capsules are long and taper pointed and suggest a heron's, or stork's bill. This plant is very common in the lawn at the head-quarters of the Wellfleet Bay Wildlife Sanctuary.

PINK SAND-SPURREY   *Spergularia rubra*   Figure 71

This little plant hugs the ground or rises only a few
inches above it. The leaves are very small, narrow and
thread-like, growing in pairs with a thin, triangular,
whitish-green covering at the point where each pair of
leaves meets the stem. The small, 5-petaled, pink flowers
blossom near the ends of the slender branchlets.

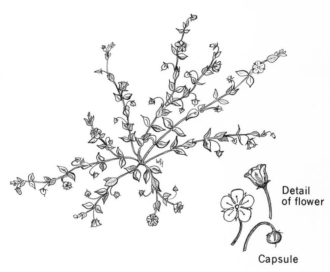

Detail
of flower

Capsule

Figure 72

SCARLET PIMPERNEL
or POORMAN'S WEATHERGLASS   *Anagallis arvensis*
Figure 72

This low, spreading plant, hardly over 10 inches tall,
has opposite, oval leaves set close to the stem. The
leaves usually have tiny, dark spots on the upper surface. The small, 5-petaled, orange-red flowers grow from
the point where leaf and main stem join. The flowers
close in dull weather, reopen in sunlight.

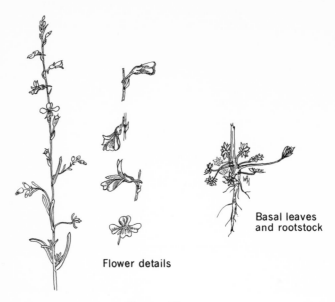

Flower details

Basal leaves
and rootstock

Figure 73

OLD-FIELD-TOADFLAX   *Linaria canadensis*   Figure 73

The 6 to 18 inch, very slender, wiry stems arising from
a rosette of small, narrow leaves, have only a few very
inconspicuous leaves along their length. Small light blue
flowers bloom near the top of the stalk.

BLUECURLS   *Trichostema dichotomum*   Figure 74

The slender, wiry stems of this 8 to 15 inch-high plant
break into pairs. The square stems are minutely hairy.
The small, opposite, aromatic leaves are oblong without
toothed margins. The flowers are dark purplish-blue
with long, yellow stamens that curl out and down.

STIFF-LEAVED ASTER   *Aster linariifolius*   Figure 75

The several stiff stems of this aster grow 4 to 12
inches high from a woody root. The numerous leaves
along the stem are narrow, rough margined and rigid.
The blue flower heads bloom singly at the ends of the
many simple branches. This low-growing aster forms
clumps of color in late August.

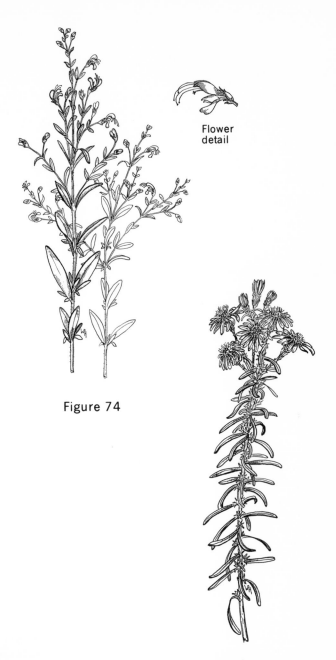

Flower
detail

Figure 74

Figure 75

PLATES

SCOTCH BROOM   *Cytisus scoparius*   Plate III, No. 1

The stiff, wiry, many branched, green stems of this 3 to 6 foot tall shrub are broom-like, giving it its common name. Most of the small leaves have three leaflets arising from a common center; some are single leaves. The showy flowers are bright yellow and are near the tips of the slender branches. The fruit is a pod, resembling a dry, flat, brown pea, with a few fine hairs along the edges.

PRICKLY PEAR CACTUS   *Opuntia humifusa*
                                        Plate III, No. 2

This is one plant never confused with any other Cape flower because of its mats of pear-shaped, or round, fleshy stems armed with a multitude of tiny barbed bristles and many longer spines. The leaves are spirally arranged, very small, awl-shaped and drop quickly from the stems. Large, bright yellow flowers, 2½ to 3 inches across, are on the tips of the stems.

ORANGE MILKWEED
or BUTTERFLY-WEED *Asclepias tuberosa* Plate III, No. 3

Clumps of rough, hairy stems, growing from a fleshy root, rise to a height of 1 to 2 feet. The leaves are narrow and lance-shaped. Clusters of brilliant orange blossoms at the top of the stems form masses of color in July. This is one of the most colorful of wildflowers. The name "butterfly-weed" may originate from its bright butterfly-like coloring or from the frequent visits of butterflies in search of nectar.

CYPRESS SPURGE *Euphorbia Cyparissias* Plate III, No. 4

This is a densely tufted, low-growing plant, 6 to 12 inches high, which forms mats of color in mid-to-late May when the beach-plum is in bloom. The light green leaves are very narrow and crowded along the stem. The flat clusters of floral leaves which resemble flowers are at the top of the stem. They are yellow or yellow-green when first formed, turning purplish or reddish as they age.

CREEPING BUTTERCUP   *Ranunculus repens*
                                       Plate III, No. 5

This hairy, creeping plant with erect flower stems often
grows in large masses. The leaves have long stems and
are 3-sectioned, with each division cleft and lobed. The 5-
petaled flowers are bright shining yellow, often an inch
or more in diameter.

BUTTER-AND-EGGS   *Linaria vulgaris*   Plate III, No. 6

The erect stems, with many narrow, pointed, closely
spaced, alternate leaves grow 1 to 2 feet high. The
flowers are two-lipped, orange and yellow, with a long
spur at the base. This plant often grows in masses,
blooming from mid-July through August.

COMMON ST. JOHN'S-WORT   *Hypericum perforatum*
                                       Plate IV, No. 1

The woody stems of this much-branched plant grow up
to 2½ feet tall. The small, opposite, somewhat oblong
leaves with rounded tips have tiny dots which show
against the light. The 5-petaled, bright yellow flowers
are in dense clusters.

EVENING-PRIMROSE   *Oenothera biennis*   Plate IV, No. 2

The stout, rank growing stems rise to a height of 1 to
4 feet. Leaves are alternate, lance-shaped, sharply
pointed, somewhat fuzzy, and frequently colored with
red. The 4-petaled, pale yellow flowers are 1 to 1½
inches in diameter. They open at dusk, remaining open
the greater part of the next day if the sun is not too
bright. Flowers are faintly fragrant and are often visited
at night by the large hawk moths.

BLACK-EYED SUSAN   *Rudbeckia hirta*   Plate IV, No. 3

This roughly hairy plant with its broad, toothed, alternate leaves, has golden yellow flower heads and a
golden brown, cone-shaped center. It resembles a large
yellow daisy, and is sometimes called by this name.

COREOPSIS   *Coreopsis lanceolata*   Plate IV, No. 4

This is another escapee from cultivation. It is erect with slender stems, 1 to 1½ feet tall. The leaves are opposite, lance-shaped, and scattered along the stem. Flower heads are daisy-like, one to a slender stem; the bright yellow rays have three notches at the tip. It is a very showy plant, especially in areas where it has become well established.

OX-EYE-DAISY   *Chrysanthemum Leucanthemum*
                                                Plate IV, No. 5

The flower heads, with their bright yellow centers and pure white rays, are borne singly on erect, wiry stems 1 to 1½ feet tall. The leaves are narrow and deeply cut along their margins. Beautiful as the large clumps of this flower may be, it can become a pernicious weed to the farmer.

YUCCA or SILKGRASS *Yucca filamentosa* Plate IV, No. 6

These are evergreen plants with long, narrow, sharp-pointed, sword-like leaves often fringed on the margins with long, thread-like fibers. The leaves are clustered, growing from a deep root. The flower stalk rises to a height of 5 to 6 feet with large, showy, drooping, creamy-white flowers.

QUEEN ANNE'S-LACE
or WILD CARROT   *Daucus Carota*   Plate V, No. 1

This tall, slender, greyish-green plant grows from 2 to 3 feet tall with very finely dissected leaves and a circular, flat-topped cluster of small white flowers. As seeds form, the flower stalks become erect, forming a cup-shaped structure somewhat resembling a bird's nest. This plant is believed to be the stock from which the garden carrot was developed.

WHITE CAMPION   *Lychnis alba*   Plate V, No. 2

This 1½ to 2 feet tall, loosely-branched plant has opposite, oval-oblong leaves arising from somewhat swollen joints of the stem. The white flowers are fragrant with heart-shaped petals that open in the evening, attracting several species of small, night-flying moths.

VIRGINIA ROSE   *Rosa virginiana*   Plate V, No. 3

The compound leaves of this rose usually have seven leaflets. The single, fragrant roses have bright yellow center stamens and five petals which vary from a light pink to a deeper color. The stems of this wild rose are thorny. The berry-like fruits, often called "hips", are bright red. Swamp rose (*Rosa palustris*) is a similar species with leaves not-toothed.

BOUNCING-BET
or SOAPWORT   *Saponaria officinalis*   Plate V, No. 4

Masses of this plant brighten roadsides and abandoned home sites with large, rose-tinged flowers at the top of the opposite-leaved stems 1 to 2 feet tall. The single form has five notched petals; the double form has many petals. Crushing the leaves in water will produce a soapy lather.

COMMON MILKWEED   *Asclepias syriaca*   Plate V, No. 5

The commonest of the milkweeds, this variety has tall, stout stems, 2 to 3 feet high with large, generally opposite, oblong, pale green leaves somewhat whitish-downy beneath. The dull purplish-pink flowers are very numerous and grow in a globular cluster at the tops of the stems. The puffy seed pods break open to release the silk tufted seeds.

CHICORY   *Cichorium Intybus*   Plate V, No. 6

These beautiful, large, clear blue flowers brighten roadsides and waste places in late summer. It is a coarse, much-branched plant, growing 1 to 2½ feet high, with lower leaves oblong, usually sharp-toothed, and partly clasping the stem. There are many small tufts of leaves along the flower stalk. The flower petals are notched at the ends.

CHAPTER FOUR

SEASHORE AND SALT MARSHES

No description is needed to define the seashore habitat. Deciding whether a lowland is a fresh or salt marsh might lead to some confusion. Fresh water marshes are undrained, whereas salt marshes have an ultimate connection with the ocean or bay, or are inundated by frequent high tides. Since the salt water source may not always be in sight, you can usually settle the matter by tasting a drop of water, although this test may not appeal to everyone.

A salt marsh has a more uniform appearance than a fresh marsh. Most of the vegetation shades into different colors and textures resembling a grassy meadow. Areas intermittently inundated, as well as larger salt ponds, may be unmarked by such zonation.

The salt marsh vegetation blooms most conspicuously in late summer and early fall. At this time, the seaside goldenrod, sea-lavender and red-tinged glassworts lend their hues to the otherwise frequently drab salt marshes.

At the edges of a salt marsh where a fresh spring or stream empties, you may find fresh marsh plants. If your specimen does not key out here, try Chapter Seven, Fresh Marshes and Meadows. Vegetation on the salt marsh banking often resembles that of Disturbed Areas, Chapter Three.

KEY TO WILDFLOWERS OF THE SEASHORE AND SALT MARSHES

a. Plant shrubby, bushy-branched with flattened leaves . . .b.

  b. Flowers conspicuous. . .c.

    c. Plant very rough and thorny; leaves dark green and shiny; flowers large, showy, purple, red or white; fruit (hip) cherry-size, bright scarlet-red, ripening in late summer: SALT-SPRAY ROSE   (*Rosa rugosa*)
Plate VI, No. 2

c. Plant not thorny. . .d.

    d. Flowers white in dense clusters before the leaves appear in spring; fruit a large-stoned, light blue to black or yellow sweet plum: BEACH-PLUM (*Prunus maritima*)   Plate VI, No. 3

    d. Flowers large, pink, with yellow center, not densely clustered; salt marsh plant blooming in late summer sometimes in upper reaches of tidal streams: ROSE-MALLOW   (*Hibiscus palustris*)   Plate VI, No. 4

b. Flowers inconspicuous. . .e.

    e. Fruit a spiny bur; leaves broad, lobed and rough; stem purple-mottled; not very tall, bushy shrub of sandy seashores: SEA-BURDOCK (*Xanthium echinatum*)   Figure 76

    e. Fruit not bur-like; leaves smooth. . .f.

        f. Flower heads nodding, greenish-white at the base of small upper leaves; lower leaves larger, fleshy, with numerous teeth; salt marshes and shores: MARSH-ELDER (*Iva frutescens*)   Figure 77

        f. Flower heads upright, scattered at ends of branches; female plants conspicuous in fruit with white, dandelion-like seed clusters; fresh or tidal marshes: SEA-MYRTLE or CONSUMPTION-WEED (*Baccharis halimifolia*)   Figure 78

a. Plant not shrubby. . .g.

    g. Flowers not conspicuously colored. . .h.

        h. Leaves with flattened lobes, silvery gray-green, hairy or velvety. . .i.

            i. Leaves silvery-white, woolly with broadly divided lobes; flowers near top of upright, leafy stalks, not showy: DUSTY MILLER (*Artemisia Stelleriana*)   Figure 79

            i. Leaves grayish-green with finely divided long, flat lobes; flowers in a tall, branching, purple-stemmed spray with greenish heads: TALL WORMWOOD (*Artemisia caudata*)   Chapter 3, Figure 40

        h. Leaves not lobed and hairy. . .j.

j. Leaves long, flat and grasslike. . .k.

   k. Plant of sandy beaches and dunes occurring in small clumps, often in a straight row from underground stems; flowers on a creamy-white spike above the leaves in late summer: BEACH-GRASS or MARRAM (*Ammophila breviligulata*)
Chapter 2, Figure 33

   k. Plants of marshlands. . .l.

      l. Very tall grass (up to 15 feet high) with bluish-green leaves and stems; flowering cluster brownish-purple, decorative; spreading rapidly by long, prostrate stems: COMMON REED (*Phragmites communis*)   Figure 80

      l. Tall plant often growing in great masses with dark brown, bottle-brush-like flower formation (cat-tail) at tip of stem, which eventually breaks up into cotton-like masses of seeds; uppermost male flowers separated from lower female flowers by a few inches, the male falling away leaving a bare spike above the female: NARROW-LEAVED CAT-TAIL (*Typha angustifolia*)   Figure 81

j. Leaves not grass-like. . .m.

   m. Plant tall (about 2 feet), with smooth, elongate, wavy-margined leaves; fruit in dry, dark brown, papery seed cases in masses at top of stem, conspicuous in late summer and autumn: WAVY-LEAVED DOCK (*Rumex crispus*)   Figure 82

   m. Plants of short height. . .n.

      n. Plants without succulent stems, stems lying flat on the sand. . .o.

         o. Leaves gray-green with white sheath at base encircling the swollen joints of the stem; flowers pink, inconspicuous in the axils of the leaves: SEABEACH KNOTWEED (*Polygonum glaucum*)   Figure 83

         o. Leaves small, long-oval; pale green, occurring in close, opposite pairs along the profusely-branched stem; SEASIDE-SPURGE (*Euphorbia polygonifolia*)   Figure 84

n.   Plants more or less succulent (fleshy). . .p.

   p.   Leaves and/or stems narrow, elongate and succulent. . .q.

      q.   Entire plant finely hairy, bush-branched, bluish-green: HAIRY BASSIA (*Bassia hirsuta*)   Figure 85

      q.   Plant smooth, not hairy. . .r.

         r.   Leaves 6 to 8 inches long, narrow, arising in a cluster from near the same spot on the root-crown; flowers greenish, inconspicuous in a spike: SEASIDE-PLANTAIN (*Plantago oliganthos*)
Figure 86

         r.   Leaves not all from the root-crown. . .s.

            s.   Jointed stems in opposite pairs, very succulent, turning reddish-orange in fall; leaves absent: GLASSWORT or SAMPHIRE (*Salicornia species*)
Figure 87

               t.   Leaves spine-tipped, dark green; mostly weak-stemmed plants of sandy seashores: SALTWORT (*Salsola Kali*)   Figure 88

               t.   Leaves soft-tipped; bluish-green or sometimes reddish and lying flat on the sand: SEA-BLITE or SEEP-WEED (*Suaeda maritima*)
Figure 89

   p.   Leaves flattened and succulent. . .u.

      u.   Leaves broad, gray-green, mealy, especially when young. . .v.

         v.   Leaves oval, wavy-margined; stem often purplish, close-branching; SEABEACH-ORACH (*Atriplex arenaria*)   Figure 90

         v.   Leaves broadly triangular (often eared at base), less mealy than the above, and less compact; weak-stemmed plant of the salt marsh borders: ORACH (*Atriplex patula*)   Figure 91

> u. Leaves bright green, bluntly attached to
> stem in opposite pairs in two ranks (ap-
> pearing squarish when viewed from
> above); plants often thickly clustered in
> sand on the seabeach, turning yellowish
> in autumn: SEABEACH-SANDWORT
> (*Arenaria peploides*)   Plate VI, No. 5

g. Flowers conspicuously colored and fitting into one of
the categories listed below:

> 1. Flowers with white petals or petal-like rays.
> 2. Flowers with blue or violet petals or petal-like
>   rays.
> 3. Flowers with red or pink petals.
> 4. Flowers with yellow petal-like rays.

1. FLOWERS WITH WHITE PETALS OR PETAL-LIKE RAYS

A. Flowers in white-rayed heads (sometimes pale purple);
leaves few, long and fleshy, pointed; plant of salt
marshes: SALINE ASTER (*Aster tenuifolius*) Figure 92

A. Flowers in compact, circular, flat-topped or rounded
clusters; leaves compound. . .B.

> B. Leaves finely divided into narrow segments; weak-
> stemmed plant of usually brackish marshes: MOCK
> BISHOP'S-WEED (*Ptilimnium capillaceum*)
>
> Figure 93

> B. Leaves with broad leaflets. . .C.

> > C. Plant tall (2½ to 4 feet); leaflets dark green, irregu-
> > larly toothed; flowers greenish-white: SEASIDE AN-
> > GELICA (*Coelopleurum lucidum*)   Figure 94

> > C. Plant shorter (1½ to 2 feet); leaflets, shiny, yellow-
> > ish-green, fleshy, regularly but coarsely toothed;
> > stems often reddish and aromatic; flowers white:
> > SCOTCH LOVAGE (*Ligusticum scothicum*)
> >
> > Figure 95

2. FLOWERS WITH BLUE OR VIOLET PETALS OR PETAL-LIKE RAYS

A. Flowers in composite heads with or without ray-like petals. . .B.

B. Flower heads violet, without petal-like rays; leaves succulent, with a strong odor of resin or camphor; borders of salt ponds and marshes: STINKWEED or SALT-MARSH FLEABANE (*Pluchea purpurascens*)
Figure 96

B. Flower heads with blue-violet to white petal-like rays; leaves long and narrow directly attached to stem; a tall bushy-branched plant with many flower heads the size of a quarter: NEW YORK ASTER (*Aster novi-belgii*)
Figure 97

A. Flowers not in composite heads. . .C.

C. Flowers tiny, in a highly-branched, wispy spray; leaves only at the base, long and rounded; found in salt marshes: SEA-LAVENDER or MARSH-ROSEMARY (*Limonium Nashii*)
Figure 98

C. Flowers larger, leaves not confined to the base. . .D.

D. Flowers symmetrical, with 4, free, light purple petals; leaves wavy-toothed, light green; fruit a rounded capsule with pointed cap: SEA-ROCKET (*Cakile edentula*)
Figure 99

D. Flowers not symmetrical, having an upper and lower lip. . .E.

E. Leaves compound with bluish-green leaflets in 4 to 10 opposite pairs; flowers purple to bluish or white, similar to garden sweet pea but smaller; vine-like plant bearing pods after the flowers have passed: BEACH-PEA or MARITIME PEA-VINE (*Lathyrus japonicus*)
Plate VI, No. 6

E. Leaves simple, opposite, soft hairy; flowers lavender or purple in a spike; stem also hairy and square angled: AMERICAN GERMANDER or WOOD-SAGE (*Teucrium canadense*)
Figure 100

3. FLOWERS WITH RED OR PINK PETALS (Low, weak-stemmed succulent plants of salt marshes)

A. Entire plant finely hairy, with small white or pinkish flowers; small triangular, papery bracts at base of the very narrow leaves: PINK SAND-SPURREY (*Spergularia rubra*)   Chapter 3, Figure 71

A. Plant smooth, flowers pink or lavender and crimson at base of leaves, leaves bluntly attached to stem in opposite pairs: SEA-MILKWORT (*Glaux maritima*)
                                                          Figure 101

4. FLOWERS WITH YELLOW PETAL-LIKE RAYS

Flowers massed in heads, bright golden-yellow in autumn; leaves large, fleshy, broadly elongate, and bluntly pointed: SEASIDE GOLDENROD (*Solidago sempervirens*)
                                         Chapter 2, Plate II, No. 1

Figure 76

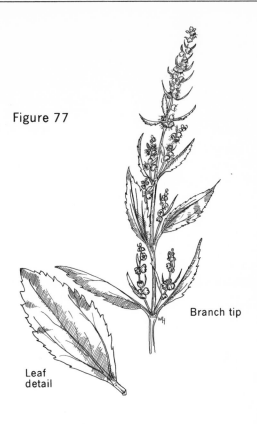

Figure 77

Branch tip

Leaf
detail

PLANT DESCRIPTIONS

SEA-BURDOCK   *Xanthium echinatum*   Figure 76

This coarse, rough, shrubby plant often has purplish or
purple-brown spotted stems. Its large leaves are very
rough with scattered hairs, finely toothed, and somewhat
lobed. In August, clusters of prickly burs are found at
the points where leaves and stems meet.

MARSH-ELDER   *Iva frutescens*   Figure 77

This plant is shrub-like at the base, from 3 to 4 feet
high, with the lower leaves lance-shaped and fleshy with
large teeth on the margins. The inconspicuous, greenish
white flower heads are nodding, and appear on the
upper parts of the stalks where leaves and stem meet.

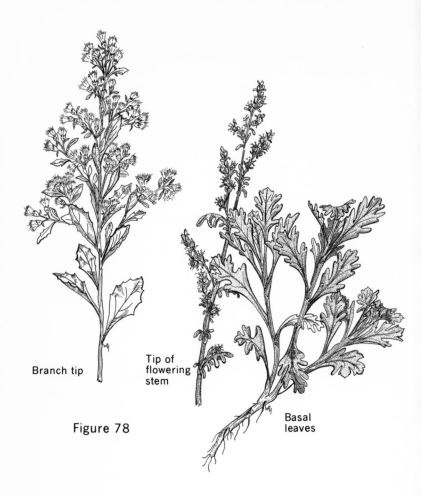

Branch tip

Tip of
flowering
stem

Figure 78

Basal
leaves

Figure 79

SEA-MYRTLE
or CONSUMPTION-WEED *Baccharis halimifolia* Figure 78

This shrub grows from 3 to 6 feet high, with oval
leaves, the lower ones toothed, and clusters of whitish
to yellowish flower heads at the ends of the branches.
In the fall, the seeds of the female shrub are very
noticeable with their large, creamy white, feathery clusters and a tuft of silk on each seed.

DUSTY MILLER   *Artemisia Stelleriana*   Figure 79

"Dusty" well describes this greenish-white, woolly plant which grows in dense clumps 1 to 2 feet high. The yellowish-to-greenish flowers are borne on upright stalks.

COMMON REED   *Phragmites communis*   Figure 80

This is a very tall grass, often 12 to 15 feet high. Its feathery, plume-like, flowering clusters are purplish-brown and very showy.

Growth habit

Figure 80

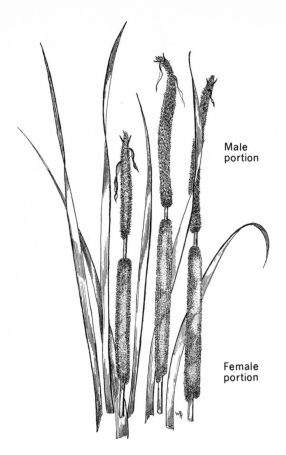

Male
portion

Female
portion

Figure 81

NARROW-LEAVED
CAT-TAIL   *Typha angustifolia*   Figure 81

Tall, growing from 3 to 4½ feet in height, with long,
narrow leaves and a stout stem bearing a cylindrical
spike with male and female flowers. In this spike the
male flowers are clustered above the reddish brown
female flowers, and are separated from them by a short
interval. The male flowers finally drop off, leaving a
short, bare spike above the bottle-brush-like female
portion.

Tip of branch

Detail
of fruit

Lower leaves

Figure 82

WAVY-LEAVED DOCK   *Rumex crispus*   Figure 82

This coarse-growing plant, often up to three feet tall, has smooth stems and leaves from 4 to 10 inches long with very wavy margins. The dark brown seeds, borne at the top of the stem in late August, are often more conspicuous than the flowers.

SEABEACH-KNOTWEED   *Polygonum glaucum*   Figure 83

A depressed, sometimes prostrate plant which seldom grows more than a few inches tall. A white, papery sheath clasps the base of each grey-green leaf where it joins the stem; small, pale pink flowers are inconspicuous.

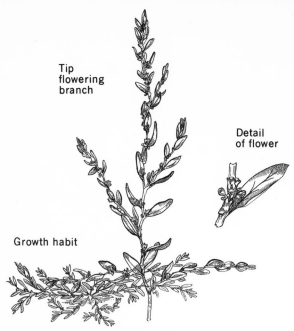

Tip
flowering
branch

Detail
of flower

Growth habit

Figure 83

SEASIDE-SPURGE   *Euphorbia polygonifolia*   Figure 84

A little, matted plant which covers a few square inches
of the sandy beach and scarcely rises above it. The
stems are smooth, sometimes quite orange-red. The pale
green leaves have a tiny point at the tip. The flowers
are small, yellowish-orange, in clusters at the ends of
the many branches.

HAIRY BASSIA   *Bassia hirsuta*   Figure 85

This plant is distinctly bluish-green and hairy, shrub-like
in growth habit and densely branched. The stems are
succulent and somewhat arching, with many small, narrow, fleshy leaves. The entire plant is seldom over a
foot high.

SEASIDE-PLANTAIN   *Plantago oliganthos*   Figure 86

The erect, fleshy, ascending leaves are long and narrow,
growing in a cluster from the top of the root. The small,
greenish flowers are in a spike frequently not as tall as
the leaves. It is a low-growing plant, usually not over a
foot in height.

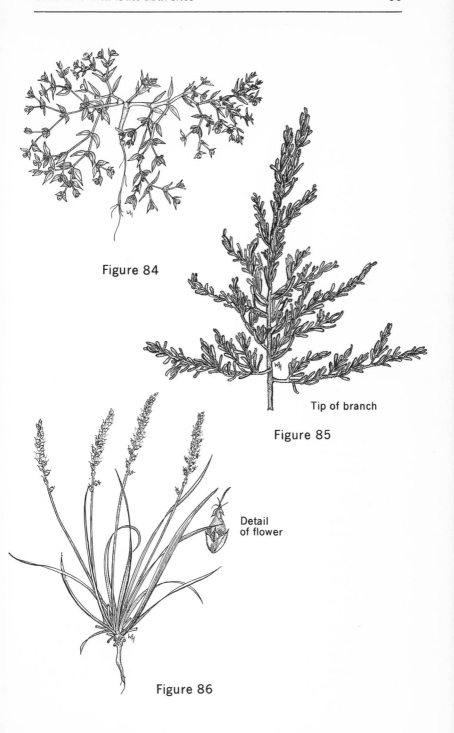

Figure 84

Tip of branch

Figure 85

Detail
of flower

Figure 86

GLASSWORT
or SAMPHIRE   *Salicornia species*   Figure 87

There are three species of glasswort on the Cape. All
are from 6 to 12 inches tall with very succulent stems
which are much-branched in opposite pairs, jointed, and
without leaves. Flowers are very tiny, pale yellow, and
appear for a short time at the upper joints of the stems.
In the fall, about the time the seaside goldenrod blooms,
considerable areas of the beach and adjacent marshes
are deep pink to salmon-red with the glassworts. Note:
The name "saltwort" is often used in reference to glassworts, but should not be confused with the true saltwort,
Salsola Kali, Figure 88.

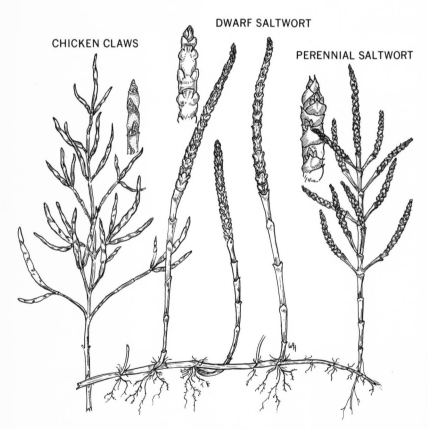

Figure 87

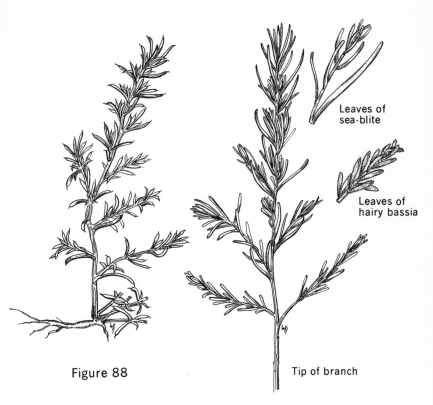

Leaves of
sea-blite

Leaves of
hairy bassia

Figure 88

Tip of branch

Figure 89

SALTWORT *Salsola Kali* Figure 88

These are branching, shrubby plants 8 to 18 inches high, with alternate, stiff, awl-shaped leaves, each tipped with a sharp spine. Small flowers, which bloom in late summer, are a pale reddish-orange and appear singly at points where leaves and stems meet. The many stiff spines make this an unsociable plant if it is brushed by the unwary bather!

SEA-BLITE or SEEPWEED *Suaeda maritima* Figure 89

Frequently found in mats close to the sand or rising not over a foot above it, this plant has bluish-green, rather soft leaves which are flattened on the upper surface and rounded beneath.

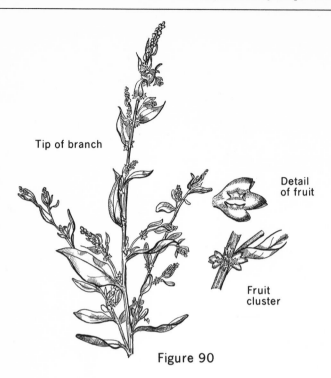

Tip of branch

Detail
of fruit

Fruit
cluster

Figure 90

SEABEACH-ORACH   *Atriplex arenaria*   Figure 90

The often purplish stems of this close-branching plant grow up to 18 inches tall, or may be found lying along the sand. The alternate, flat leaves are grey-green.

ORACH   *Atriplex patula*   Figure 91

The triangular leaves, often with a projecting lobe at either side of the base, will distinguish this 1 to 2 foot-high plant. The stem is so weak that the plant frequently trails along the ground. Small purplish flowers appear in clusters at the tips of the upper branches.

SALINE ASTER   *Aster tenuifolius*   Figure 92

The smooth, single, occasional forking stem rises from 6 to 12 inches. The few, pale green leaves are long, narrow and pointed. The small white-to-pale purple flowers grow at the top of the stem. This inconspicuous little aster blooms partially concealed by the stiff marsh grasses with which it grows.

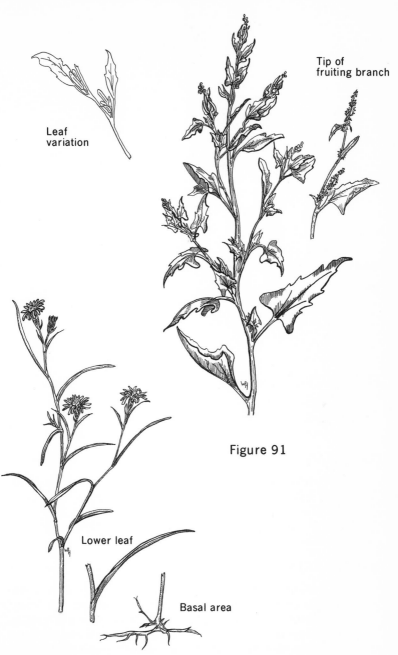

Leaf
variation

Tip of
fruiting branch

Figure 91

Lower leaf

Basal area

Figure 92

Figure 93

MOCK BISHOP'S-WEED *Ptilimnium capillaceum* Figure 93

This feathery, delicate plant is variable in height, growing from 1½ to 3 feet tall, with branching stems. The
leaves are cut into fine, thread-like divisions. The very
small, white flowers grow in a cluster at the ends of
the stems.

SEASIDE ANGELICA   *Coelopleurum lucidum*   Figure 94

Tall, stout-stemmed and rank-growing, this plant often
reaches a height of 4 feet. The compound leaves are
large with broad, dark green, irregularly toothed leaflets
and have inflated leaf stems. The flowers are white or
greenish in large, spreading clusters at the top of the
stem.

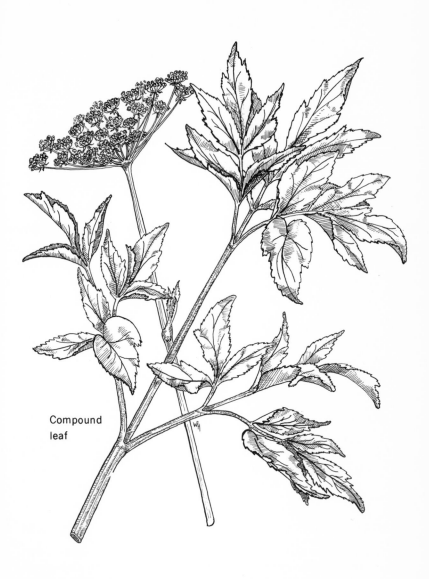

Compound
leaf

Figure 94

Figure 95

SCOTCH LOVAGE   *Ligusticum scothicum*   Figure 95

This plant is somewhat similar to the preceding species, but is shorter, usually not over 2 feet tall. The compound leaves are not divided into as many lobes, and the teeth are regular. The stem is scarcely branched, usually reddish-purple at the base. The white flowers are in flat topped clusters.

STINKWEED
or SALT-MARSH FLEABANE   *Pluchea purpurascens*
                                                  Figure 96

The pale purple flower heads, without rays, and the camphor-like odor should identify this plant. It is 1 to 2 feet tall, with pale green, succulent leaves growing close to the stem. The pond at the Wellfleet Wildlife Sanctuary is bordered with a thick stand of this plant and is quite colorful when it flowers in late July.

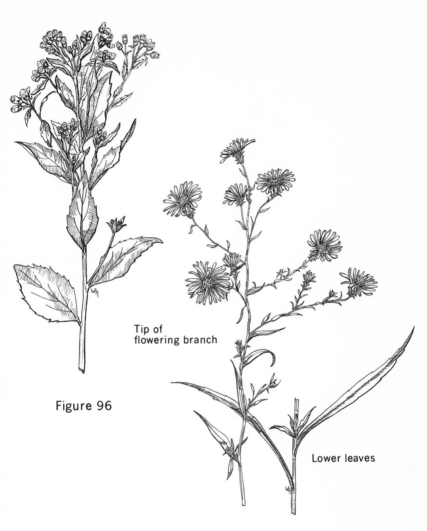

Tip of
flowering branch

Figure 96

Lower leaves

Figure 97

NEW YORK ASTER   *Aster novi-belgii*   Figure 97

A tall, slender, much-branched aster, growing from 1½
to 3 feet high, with long, narrow leaves, the upper ones
partly clasping the stem. The large flower heads vary
in color from blue-violet to almost white. It is found in
damp thickets late in the fall.

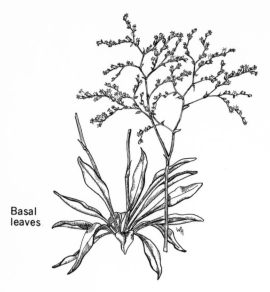

Basal
leaves

Figure 98

SEA-LAVENDER
or MARSH-ROSEMARY   *Limonium Nashii*   Figure 98

The single, stiff, leafless stem of this plant, rising 1 to 2
feet high, breaks into a spray-like cluster of many small
branchlets each covered with tiny, pale lavender flowers
in mid-to-late August. The thick, oblong leaves with
rounded tips and long stems grow in a cluster directly
from the root; they are dark green, often suffused with
red.

SEA-ROCKET   *Cakile edentula*   Figure 99

A fleshy plant of the sandy beach above the high tide
mark, growing from 6 to 12 inches in height, with the
lower branches spreading and the center one erect. The
leaves are grey-green, sometimes lobed, wavy toothed
and narrowed at the base. The small flowers are light
purple with four long-clawed petals. The jointed seed
capsules are distinctive, with the upper joint longer than
the lower and narrowed into a beak. The lower joint is
rounded.

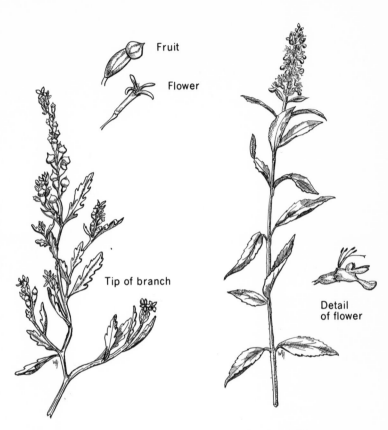

Fruit

Flower

Tip of branch

Detail of flower

Figure 100

Figure 99

AMERICAN GERMANDER
or WOOD-SAGE   *Teucrium canadense*   Figure 100

The stiff, hairy, 4-angled stem of this plant rises to a height of 9 to 18 inches with short stemmed, lance-shaped leaves which are hairy beneath. The flowers are pale lavender or purple in a terminal spike. The irregularly-shaped flower has two upright upper lobes and three broader, descending lower ones.

Detail of flower

Figure 101

SEA-MILKWORT   *Glaux maritima*   Figure 101

The loosely ascending branches of this small plant, 6 to
15 inches high, are frequently intertwined with the
marsh grasses with which it grows. The small, narrow
leaves are arranged in opposite pairs and are without
leaf stems. The flowers are small, 5-parted bells and
bloom where leaf and stem meet. The flower colors vary
from white through pink and lavender to a light crimson.

PLATES

SALTSPRAY ROSE   *Rosa rugosa*   Plate VI, No. 2

This rough, very thorny, shrubby plant, often grows in
dense clumps several feet in diameter and 6 feet high.
The compound leaves have 5 to 9 dark green leaflets,
lighter beneath, with heavy veins on the upper surface.
The gorgeous, 5-petaled, rose purple flowers, single, and
often 4 inches in diameter, are on short bristly stems.
The fruit is a bright scarlet, cherry size "hip" which
makes excellent jelly.

BEACH-PLUM *Prunus maritima* Plate VI, No. 3

Some of the shrubs are low and straggling, others ascend to a height of 6 feet; all are many-branched. The
dense clusters of small, 5-petaled white flowers cover the
branches before the leaves appear. The fruit varies from
light blue to almost black; a yellow-fruited form is sometimes found. The beach-plum flower display in late May
through early June is one of the finest of any season on
the Cape. Its fruit is the source of the famous Cape Cod
Beach-plum jelly.

ROSE-MALLOW *Hibiscus palustris* Plate VI, No. 4

This coarse growing plant often reaches a height of 4 to
5 feet. The large oval, toothed leaves, slightly heart-
shaped at the base, are covered with many fine white
hairs on the under surface. The late summer blooming
flowers are very showy, with their five deep rose petals
and bright yellow centers.

SEABEACH-SANDWORT *Arenaria peploides*
Plate VI, No. 5

This plant grows in mats 6 to 15 inches tall, often covering an area of several square feet. Its elliptic leaves are
a bright yellow-green, without stems, growing in opposite pairs at right angles to each other thus giving the
plant a square appearance when viewed from above.
The flowering tips, with their yellowish flowers, are
usually somewhat branched.

BEACH-PEA
or MARITIME PEA-VINE *Lathyrus japonicus*
Plate VI, No. 6

This is a vine-like plant 1 to 2 feet long with leaves and
flower stems ascending from 6 to 12 inches above the
sand. The leaves are compound, with 4 to 10 opposite
leaflets; the central stem of these leaves ends in a tendril. The flowers are like those of a sweet pea, varying
in color from almost-white to a deep blue-purple. A rose-
colored form is sometimes found. The fruit resembles a
garden pea, although somewhat flatter.

CHAPTER FIVE

POND AREAS

Cape Cod is well provided with lakes and ponds. Most of them are deep and sandy-margined, although a few are shallow and muddy. The plants in these two general types of watery areas differ considerably, but will not be separated in the key itself. Aquatic types grow completely under water, or float or emerge above the water; these are all common in the muddier ponds. The sandy margins of the deeper ponds support a rich and colorful flora especially in late summer.

Most of the ponds are called kettle-holes. Geologists explain that as a glacier retreated northward about 15,000 years ago, huge chunks of ice which remained buried in the debris slowly melted, leaving these depressions. Ground water now fills them to depths that vary according to the size of the ice chunk and to the elevation of the pond.

The wind-circulated shore currents have given many of these ponds circular shapes. The currents carry sand from the headlands to the bays, or even cut off the deeper bays with arms of sand. The shore of the Great Pond in Wellfleet provides a dramatic example of this contouring. While walking there or consulting a topographic map, notice how the irregular outline has been rounded off leaving a pond at the four corners. The satellite ponds vary in depth; one may be almost completely dried while another is boggy.

Not all ponds are glacial remains. Those of the Province Lands and those on the larger sand spits such as Nauset beach and Monomoy Island represent low areas between old dunes, where the pond surface shows the water table for the area. Shallower and muddier than the kettle-hole ponds, they favor a different vegetation. In early spring bright yellow spikes of golden club, a relative of jack-in-the-pulpit, skunk cabbage and sweetflag fill some ponds in the Province Lands, while in late summer others are crowded with white water-lilies.

The vegetation of the bog ponds, those ponds surrounded by dense shrubbery or quaking mats of peat moss, is keyed in Chapter Six, Boglands. Similarly the vegetation of the salt ponds is keyed in Chapter Four, Seashore and Salt Marshes.

KEY TO WILDFLOWERS OF THE POND AREAS

a. Plants found growing in open water, or near the water's edge. . .b.

b. Shrubby plants. . .c.

   c. Upright branching shrub with white ball-shaped clusters of flowers: BUTTONBUSH (*Cephalanthus occidentalis*)   Plate VII, No. 1

   c. Arching shrub with wand-like branches; lavender flowers clustered at base of leaves: WATER-WILLOW or SWAMP-LOOSESTRIFE (*Decodon verticillatus*)   Plate VII, No. 2

b. Not shrubby; upright or floating plants. . .d.

   d. Plants free floating, without leaves; tiny bladder-like animal traps on underwater branches; 1 or 2 purple flowers on upright stalks: PURPLE BLADDERWORT (*Utricularia purpurea*)   Figure 102

   d. Plants rooted to bottom. . .e.

      e. Leaves usually floating. . .f.

         f. Flowers white. . .g.

           g. Flowers tiny, delicate; leaves about 1 to 1.5 inches long, heart-shaped: FLOATING-HEART (*Nymphoides cordata*)   Figure 103

           g. Flowers large, showy; leaves much larger: WHITE WATER-LILY (*Nymphaea odorata*)   Plate VII, No. 3

         f. Flowers yellow: YELLOW POND-LILY (*Nuphar variegatum*)   Plate VII, No. 4

      e. Leaves not floating, occurring either above or below the water surface. . .h.

         h. Leaves extending above the water's surface. . .i.

           i. Flowers white or yellow. . .j.

      j. Flowers white. . .k.

         k. Flowers in dense, rounded clusters; male and female clusters separate; leaves alternate, reed-like, with sheathing base; fruit a spiny ball: BUR-REED (*Sparganium americanum*)   Figure 104

         k. Flowers separate, 3-petaled. . .l.

            l. Leaves large, arrowhead or lance-shaped; WAPATO or DUCK POTATO (*Sagittaria latifolia*)   Figure 105

            l. Leaves without a flattened blade, narrow, cylindrical and septate: SLENDER ARROWHEAD (*Sagittaria teres*)   Figure 105

      j. Flowers golden-yellow, embedded in a fleshy spike; leaves large, elongate and round-tipped, blue-green absent when flowering in early spring: GOLDEN CLUB (*Orontium aquaticum*)   Plate VII, No. 5

    i. Flowers small, blue-violet, orchid-like, in a short, dense, spike; leaves elongate, blunt heart-shaped: PICKERELWEED (*Pontederia cordata*)   Plate VII, No. 6

  h. Leaves clustered at base of flower stalk, often submerged at water's edge. . .m.

      m. Flowers small, pale violet, drooping, several along the stalk which extends above water: WATER-LOBELIA (*Lobelia Dortmanna*)   Figure 106

      m. Flowers snowy-white tightly clustered in a button-like disk at top of stalk: PIPEWORT (*Eriocaulon septangulare*)   Figure 107

a. Plants growing well above water's edge, on upper beach or in low, muddy areas along shore. . .n.

  n. Leaves covered with sticky, reddish hairs. . .o.

    o. Flowers small, white. . .p.

      p. Leaves circular: ROUNDED-LEAVED SUNDEW (*Drosera rotundifolia*)   Figure 108

   p.   Leaves spoon-shaped: SPOON-LEAVED SUNDEW
        (*Drosera intermedia*)   Figure 108

  o.   Flowers pink, larger: THREAD-LEAVED SUNDEW
       (*Drosera filiformis*)   Figure 108

n.   Leaves not covered with sticky, reddish hairs. . .q.

 q.   Flowers white or yellow. . .r.

   r.   Flowers white. . .s.

     s.   Tall, rough-hairy plants with opposite leaves
          united around the stem; flowers in closely-packed
          clusters: BONESET (*Eupatorium perfoliatum*)
                                                Figure 109

     s.   Low growing plant with weak and reclining
          stems; leaves rounded with scalloped edges;
          flowers in small, domed clusters: WATER-
          PENNYWORT (*Hydrocotyle umbellata*)
                                                Figure 110

   r.   Flowers yellow. . .t.

     t.   Flowers in large, flat-topped clusters; leaves
          long and narrow; GRASS-LEAVED GOLDEN-
          ROD (*Solidago tenuifolia*)   Chapter 3, Figure 51

     t.   Flowers not tightly clustered. . .u.

       u.   Plants low, usually in masses; petals united
            to form a 5-lobed tube, like a small snap-
            dragon: GOLDEN-PERT (*Gratiola aurea*)
                                                Figure 111

       u.   Plants taller, more scattered. . .v.

         v.   Flowers 3-petaled; leaves grass-like from
              the base: YELLOW-EYED-GRASS (*Xyris
              Congdoni*)   Figure 112

         v.   Flowers 5-petaled; less than 1½ inch across;
              capsules red or purple. . .w.

           w.   Leaves rounded: NORTHERN ST.
                JOHN'S-WORT (*Hypericum boreale*)
                                                Figure 113

           w.   Leaves narrow: CANADA ST. JOHN'S-
                WORT (*Hypericum canadense*) Figure 114

q.   Flowers pink or purple. . .x.

x.   Flowers pink. . .y.

y.   Flowers small, tightly clustered. . .z.

z.   Tall, soft-hairy plant with opposite leaves;
fruit a large pod with silky seed attachments:
SWAMP-MILKWEED (*Asclepias incarnata*)
Plate VIII, No. 1

z.   Low plant with narrow, whorled leaves and
tiny, clustered orchid-like flowers with yellow
centers: CROSS-LEAVED MILKWORT (*Poly-
gala cruciata*)   Figure 115

y.   Flowers large, not tightly clustered. . .aa.

aa.   Flowers occurring in heads; leaves narrow;
petal-like rays pale lavender or white;
flower center yellow-brown: TICKSEED or
ROSE COREOPSIS (*Coreopsis rosea*)
Figure 116

aa.   Flowers not occurring in heads. . .bb.

bb.   Flowers with 8 to 12 petals, pink with
yellow centers; often occurring in large
colonies, handsome: PLYMOUTH GEN-
TIAN   or   SABATIA (*Sabatia Ken-
nedyana*)   Plate VIII, No. 2

bb.   Flowers with 4 or 5 petals leaves opposite. . .cc.

cc.   Petals 5, pointed; leaves rounded, dull
green, whitish beneath: MARSH ST.
JOHN'S-WORT   (*Hypericum virgini-
cum*)   Figure 117

cc.   Petals 4, rounded; leaves oval-pointed:
MEADOW-BEAUTY or DEERGRASS
(*Rhexia virginica*)   Figure 118

x.   Flowers purple; petals united to form a tube like a
snapdragon; leaves narrow, often purple tinged:
PURPLE GERARDIA (*Gerardia purpurea*)
Figure 119

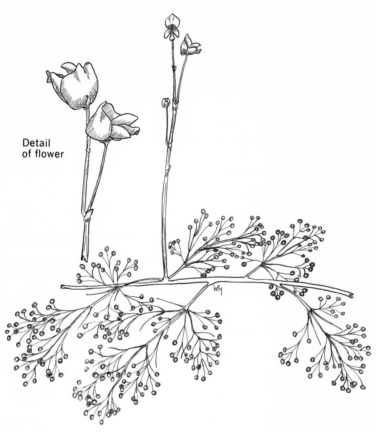

Detail
of flower

Figure 102

PLANT DESCRIPTIONS

PURPLE BLADDERWORT *Utricularia purpurea* Figure 102

This plant floats freely, often forming mats several square feet in area that move wherever they are blown by the wind. The immersed part of the plant is thread-like and bears upright flower stems which project above the water, each bearing 2 to 5 purple, or deep pink flowers. The underwater "bladders" are traps for catching tiny, microscopic animals for food.

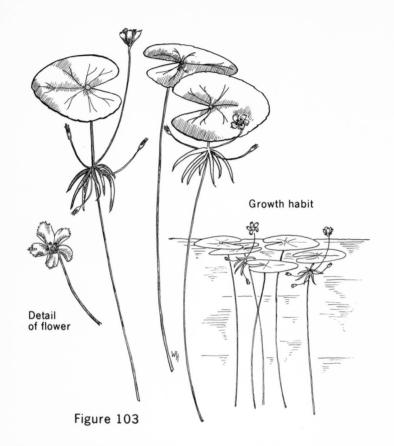

Growth habit

Detail
of flower

Figure 103

FLOATING-HEART   *Nymphoides cordata*   Figure 103

This floating plant might be described as a very tiny
water-lily. Its dainty, heart-shaped leaves, scarcely more
than an inch broad, are attached to long stems rooted to
the bottom. The tiny, white, 5-petaled flowers are raised
just above the water and have a cluster of aquatic roots
where the flower stem branches from the leaf stem.

BUR-REED   *Sparganium americanum*   Figure 104

This inhabitant of the muddy pond shores grows 10 to 18
inches tall with reed-like leaves clasping the flowering
stem. The greenish-white flowers are in ball-shaped
clusters, with male and female flowers separated. The
flower clusters are about an inch in diameter. The fruit
is spiny and globe-shaped.

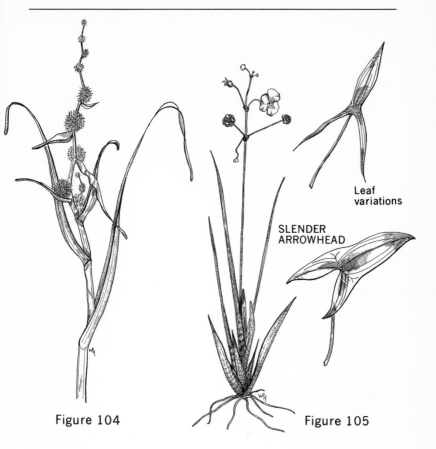

Leaf
variations

SLENDER
ARROWHEAD

Figure 104   Figure 105

WAPATO or DUCK POTATO *Sagittaria latifolia* Figure 105

The leaves are long-stemmed, clasping at the base, arrow-shaped, with triangular basal lobes. The leaves are quite variable, some much narrower than the typical broader form. Showy, white flowers with bright yellow centers have three petals arranged in whorls of three on a leafless stem 1 to 2½ feet high.

SLENDER ARROWHEAD   *Sagittaria teres*   Figure 105

Flowers of this arrowhead are similar to the preceding species, although smaller. It grows in the water with its very narrow, spongy, tubular leaves divided into crosswise partitions projecting above the surface 6 to 12 inches.

WATER-LOBELIA   *Lobelia Dortmanna*   Figure 106

Many ponds have dozens of these stiff-stemmed, leafless flower stalks, with their pale bluish-white, drooping flowers rising 6 to 12 inches above the water a few feet from the edge. The narrow leaves are in an underwater cluster at the base of the flower stalks. This plant is a close relative of the brilliant, red cardinal-flower.

PIPEWORT   *Eriocaulon septangulare*   Figure 107

This plant is well described by one of its common names, "white buttons." The small, white flower clusters are button-like, borne on a single stem 2 to 6 inches above the water level. The leaves are beneath the water, awl-shaped at the base of the flower stems. This little plant grows profusely along the shallow edges of many ponds.

ROUND-LEAVED SUNDEW   *Drosera rotundifolia*
Figure 108

Sundews grow in muddy areas above the high water mark of ponds, or in boggy spots along their shores. All have sticky, reddish hairs with drops of liquid on them. These leaves catch and "digest" insects as a source of the nitrogen they need for plant food, largely lacking in the soil in which they grow. The small leaves of this species are round, abruptly narrowed into spreading hairy stalks and grow in a cluster from 1 to 4 inches in diameter close to the ground. Flowers are small, white, on an erect stem 4 to 6 inches tall.

SPOON-LEAVED SUNDEW *Drosera intermedia* Figure 108

Very similar to the preceding species, but, as its name implies, it has narrowed, distinctly spoon-shaped leaves.

THREAD-LEAVED SUNDEW *Drosera filiformis* Figure 108

This sundew has very slender, thread-like leaves 4 to 10 inches tall, densely covered with sticky hairs. The flowers are pale purplish-pink on an erect stem somewhat taller than the leaves. Under proper conditions, usually in moist sand, this plant often covers considerable areas just above the high water mark.

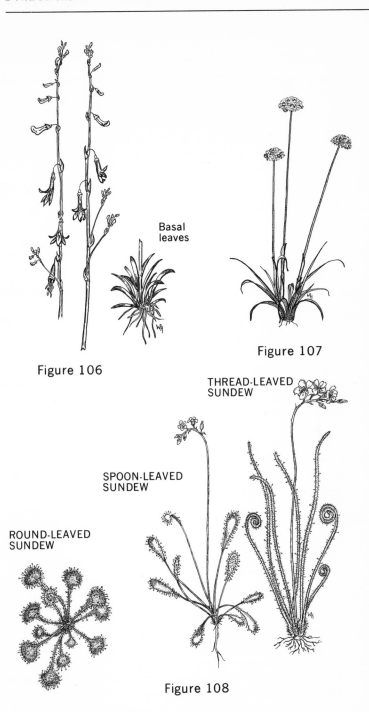

Basal
leaves

Figure 106

Figure 107

THREAD-LEAVED
SUNDEW

SPOON-LEAVED
SUNDEW

ROUND-LEAVED
SUNDEW

Figure 108

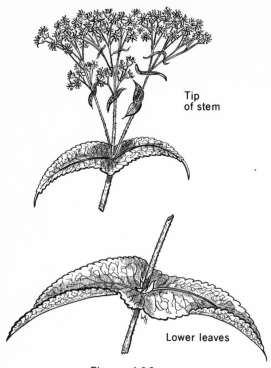

Tip
of stem

Lower leaves

Figure 109

BONESET   *Eupatorium perfoliatum*   Figure 109

This coarse-growing plant rises to 3 to 4 feet in height
with opposite, roughly hairy, toothed and wavy-edged
leaves joining at their base to clasp the stem. The grey-
ish-white flowers are in dense, flat-topped clusters at
the top of the stem and the ends of any side branches.

WATER-PENNYWORT   *Hydrocotyle umbellata*   Figure 110

This small, weak-growing plant of the sandy pond edges
is 4 to 6 inches tall, with domed clusters of white
flowers at the top of the stem. The distinctive leaves
are round, with scalloped edges ½ to 1½ inches in
diameter, and a long, slender stem attached toward the
center of the under surface. This plant commonly grows
and blooms with the rosy coreopsis and the Plymouth
gentian in late July and early August.

Figure 110   Figure 111

GOLDEN-PERT   *Gratiola aurea*   Figure 111

This small plant grows from creeping stems which ascend
3 to 6 inches, with light, yellow-green leaves which are
partly clasping. The clear yellow, tubular flowers form
masses of color along the sandy pond margins from mid-
July to mid-August. The front end of the flower is two-
lipped; the upper section without divisions, the lower
cut into three lobes.

YELLOW-EYED-GRASS   *Xyris Congdoni*   Figure 112

This small, tufted plant has flat, long, grass-like leaves
4 to 10 inches tall, growing in a clump from numerous
fibrous roots. The buds look like small, yellowish beads
and open into yellow, 3-petaled flowers borne at the tip
of wiry stems, usually a few inches taller than the
leaves.

NORTHERN ST. JOHN'S-WORT   *Hypericum boreale*
                                              Figure 113

These small, slender plants are 6 to 12 inches tall, much-branched above the middle, with opposite, oval, stemless leaves. The very small, 5-petaled, yellow flowers are on loose sprays at the ends of the branches. The seed capsules are purplish-red.

CANADA ST. JOHN'S-WORT   *Hypericum canadense*
                                              Figure 114

This plant even slenderer than the preceding species, is often found associated with it. The erect stems are 6 to 12 inches high with a few branches near the top. The leaves are opposite, narrow, lance-shaped. The very small yellow flowers, with 5 petals are at the ends of the branches. Seed capsules are purplish red.

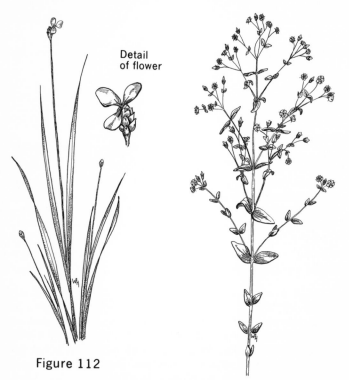

Detail
of flower

Figure 112

Figure 113

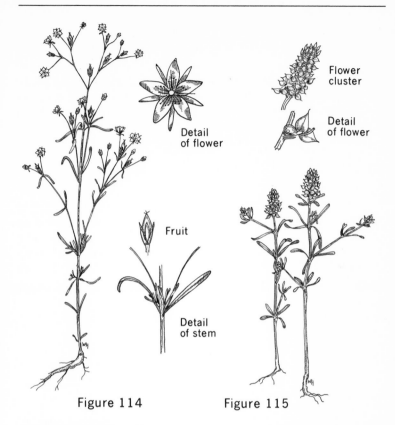

Detail
of flower

Flower
cluster

Detail
of flower

Fruit

Detail
of stem

Figure 114   Figure 115

CROSS-LEAVED MILKWORT *Polygala cruciata* Figure 115

This is a rather inconspicuous plant of the sandy pond edges, growing 4 to 6 inches high. The stems are square with whorls of four narrow leaves. The tiny, purplish or sometimes greenish-purple flowers are in a tight spike at the top of the stem and its few branches.

TICKSEED
or ROSE COREOPSIS   *Coreopsis rosea*   Figure 116

This is a small plant, 6 to 12 inches tall, with an erect, wiry, branching stem and opposite, very narrow, stemless leaves. The pale rose, lavender, sometimes white flower heads have petal-like rays surrounding a yellow-brown center. The rays of the older flowers hang down, a characteristic which, together with its much smaller size, distinguishes it from the Plymouth Gentian with which it is commonly found in mid-July to mid-August.

Figure 116   Figure 117

MARSH ST. JOHN'S-WORT   *Hypericum virginicum*
                                             Figure 117

This erect, smooth, branching plant, 6 to 12 inches high, has opposite, elliptical, dark green leaves rounded at both ends. The leaves are lighter beneath, with many fine dark dots. The 5-petaled, flesh-colored to pinkish-purple flowers are at the tips of the branching stems and also at points where leaves and stem meet. The en-entire plant often has a pinkish tinge. The seed capsules are deep red and conspicuous.

MEADOW-BEAUTY
or DEERGRASS   *Rhexia virginica*   Figure 118

The stem of this stiffly erect plant, 8 to 12 inches tall,

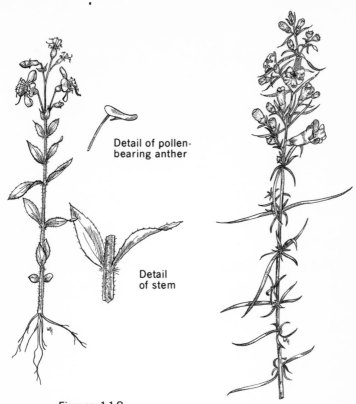

Detail of pollen-bearing anther

Detail of stem

Figure 118

Figure 119

is 4-angled with small bristles, particularly at points where the leaves and stem meet. The leaves are oval with rounded bases and are attached directly to the stem. The 4-petaled flowers are about an inch in diameter, blooming one or two at a time at the top of the stem. The flowers appear from mid-July to mid-August.

PURPLE GERARDIA   *Gerardia purpurea*   Figure 119

The wide-branching stem is 9 to 18 inches tall with long, narrow, opposite, pointed leaves. The bright, purplish-pink flowers are tubular, swelling above to five more or less unequal lobes. The entire plant is often tinged with purple. These plants often make a very showy display in early August.

PLATES

BUTTONBUSH   *Cephalanthus occidentalis*   Plate VII, No. 1

When in flower in mid-August, this shrub is easily identified by its white, globular flower heads. The oval
leaves are opposite, sometimes in 3 to 4 whorls. They
are a lustrous, bright green above; lighter, and somewhat hairy beneath. The branches are 4-sided and frequently reddish at the tips.

WATER-WILLOW
or SWAMP-LOOSESTRIFE   *Decodon verticillatus*
                                Plate VII, No. 2

Thickets of this shrubby plant, 2 to 4 feet high, with
long, arching sprays are common around many pond
edges. The leaves are opposite or in whorls, lance-
shaped, and grow close to the branches. Clusters of 5-
petaled, pinkish purple flowers bloom where the leaves
and stems meet.

WHITE WATER-LILY   *Nymphaea odorata*   Plate VII, No. 3

The circular, notched "pads" often cover the surface of
many ponds, especially in the Province Lands. The many-
petaled, very fragrant, ivory white flowers with their
central cluster of bright, orange-yellow stamens are a
familiar sight from mid-July through mid-August. The
stems are long and rubbery, reaching down to roots
often 1 to 3 feet beneath the surface.

YELLOW POND-LILY   *Nuphar variegatum*   Plate VII, No. 4

This is a coarser plant than the white water-lily. Its
leaves are notched and have rounded lobes at the base
where the stem is attached. The leaf midrib is raised
and extends as a ridge down the stem. The large, yellow, globe-shaped flowers have fleshy, incurved petals
and are borne singly on a stem a few inches above the
water.

GOLDEN CLUB *Orontium aquaticum* Plate VII, No. 5

The bright yellow, club-like flower columns rise 10 to 15 inches above the water in early spring, before the leaves appear. When the large leaves appear, they are a dark, blue-green, without teeth or lobes, projecting just above the water or floating if the water level is high. When water level is low, the large, fleshy rootstocks are seen growing in the mud. Several ponds in the Province Lands have quantities of this unusual plant.

PICKERELWEED *Pontederia cordata* Plate VII, No. 6

Each stout stem rising above the water is topped with only one long, thick, glossy, dark green leaf. These are arrow-or heart-shaped, without teeth, and pointed at the tip. Dark blue-violet flowers are in a close spike on an erect stem with one leaf attached, and rise 1 to 2½ feet above the surface. Many pond edges are blue with this flower in August.

SWAMP-MILKWEED *Asclepias incarnata* Plate VIII, No. 1

This tall, branching plant, 2 to 4 feet high, has minute, soft hairs on the upper part of the stem. The numerous leaves are narrowly oblong, pointed at the tip, and without stems. The bright purple-pink flowers are in loose clusters at the ends of the branches. An erect pod contains the seeds with their silky attachments for wind distribution. Blooming time is late July through August.

PLYMOUTH GENTIAN
or SABATIA *Sabatia Kennedyana* Plate VIII, No. 2

The beautiful, delicately fragrant, deep rose pink flowers with yellow centers form a branching spray on erect, smooth, slender stems. The flowering stems rise from a rosette of leaves close to the ground and have narrow, pointed, lance-shaped leaves along their length. This plant often grows in great numbers along the sandy shores of many ponds making them pink with bloom in mid-July through mid-August. A white-flowered form is sometimes found. The common form is shown on the front cover of this book.

CHAPTER SIX

BOGLANDS

If, when you are kneeling beside a flower in an open low-land, the ground or moss quakes beneath you or if the ground is covered with a small, oval-leaved, loosely-matted, trailing plant (cranberry), then you know you are in one of two types of bogs. Springy and very wet, the quaking bog may entirely cover or merely border a pond; its soil appears almost liquid. The cranberry bog develops in moist lowlands between dunes, or in lowlands of active or abandoned cranberry cultivation. The soil here is usually sandy loam. The quaking bog is the more interesting, though it can be dangerous if you happen to step through the floating mats of vegetation.

Soil in these boglands is very acid because bacterial or fungal decay cannot release many of the nitrates and phosphates needed as plant nutrients. In such an environment, several plants have evolved intricate methods for entrapping animal organisms, using them as fertilizer. The sundew, pitcher-plant and bladderwort digest insects for this purpose.

Neither kind of bog is particularly rare, but when found after careful searching, each reveals its characteristic flora. Look for cranberry bogs where ditches have been cut through lowlands, or along the margins of swampy ponds. In the Province Lands at the tip of the Cape look for them in the moist lowlands between the dunes.

At the edges of a salt marsh, where a fresh spring or stream empties, you may find fresh marsh plants. If your specimen does not key out here, try Chapter Seven, Fresh Marshes and Meadows. Vegetation on the salt marsh banking often resembles that of Disturbed Areas, Chapter Three.

KEY TO WILDFLOWERS OF THE BOGLANDS

a.   Flowers and/or leaves red, rose or lavender. . .b.

    b.   Leaves reddish or red-streaked when full grown. . .c.

    c. Hollow-leaved plant with red-petaled, nodding flowers: PITCHER-PLANT (*Sarracenia purpurea*)
Plate VIII, No. 3

    c. Glistening, sticky-leaved plant with small white flowers: SPOON-LEAVED SUNDEW (*Drosera intermedia*)   Chapter 5, Figure 108

  b. Leaves normally green. . .d.

    d. Entire plant with only one flower. . .e.

      e. Leaves one, grass-like: ARETHUSA or SWAMP-PINK (*Arethusa bulbosa*)   Plate VIII, No. 4

      e. Leaves two, one on the stem and a smaller one near the flower: ROSE POGONIA or SNAKE'S-MOUTH ORCHID (*Pogonia ophioglossoides*)
Figure 120

    d. Plant with several flowers. . .f.

      f. Plant with only one grass-like leaf; flowers lavender with yellow-spotted upper petals: GRASS-PINK (*Calopogon pulchellus*)   Plate VIII, No. 5

      f. Plant with many leaves. . .g.

        g. Leaves arranged on each side of the stem opposite each other. . .h.

          h. Flowers 4-petaled, not clustered; stem with winged edges less than one foot high: DEER-GRASS or MEADOW-BEAUTY (*Rhexia virginica*)   Chapter 5, Figure 118

          h. Flowers 5-petaled, smaller, closely clustered at top of stem; leaves soft, hairy beneath; taller plant: SWAMP-MILKWEED (*Asclepias incarnata*)   Chapter 5, Plate VIII, No. 1

        g. Leaves arranged several from one place on the stem (whorled); flowers lavender, clustered at base of leaves; plant short, shrubby, with arching, wand-like branches and spongy base: WATER-WILLOW or SWAMP-LOOSESTRIFE (*Decodon verticillatus*) Chapter 5, Plate VII, No. 2

a. Flowers blue, white or yellow. . .i.

  i. Plants small, low and trailing with small white and pink flowers and bright red globular fruits. . .j.

j. Leaves strongly whitened beneath: DWARF CRAN-
BERRY (*Vaccinium Oxycoccos*)   Figure 121

j. Leaves only pale beneath, larger: AMERICAN CRAN-
BERRY (*Vaccinium macrocarpon*)   Figure 121

i. Plants larger, not trailing. . .k.

  k. Flowers bright yellow. . .l.

    l. Leaves apparently absent from stem; plant about
6 inches tall; flowers with a nectar spur: HORNED
BLADDERWORT (*Utricularia cornuta*) Figure 122

    l. Leaves several. . .m.

      m. Leaves grass-like; flowers with 3 wrinkled petals
from a rounded head at top of stem: YELLOW-
EYED GRASS (*Xyris Congdoni*)
                        Chapter 5, Figure 112

      m. Leaves extending along an upright flower stem,
becoming progressively smaller toward the top;
flowers in a one-sided cluster: BOG GOLDEN-
ROD (*Solidago uliginosa*)   Figure 123

  k. Flowers blue or white. . .n.

    n. Flowers or fruiting head white. . .o.

      o. Leaves floating, flowers large with yellow cen-
ter: WHITE WATER-LILY (*Nymphaea odorata*)
                    Chapter 5, Plate VII, No. 3

      o. Leaves otherwise. . .p.

        p. Fruiting head of plant similar to cotton-boll:
COTTON-GRASS (*Eriophorum virginicum*)
                           Figure 124

        p. Plant not as above. . .q.

          q. Leaves divided into three long leaflets; flow-
ers in upright cluster in spring; plant trailing in wetter spots: BOGBEAN (*Menyanthes
trifoliata*)   Figure 125

          q. Leaves broad, not divided. . .r.

            r. Plant shrubby; flowers very fragrant; buds
pinkish, sticky; leaves shiny: SWAMP A-
ZALEA (*Rhododendron viscosum*)
                           Figure 126

r. Plant low, fleshy leaves broadly arrow-head-shaped; flowers embedded in a white, fleshy spike (spadix) surrounded by a green (internally white) pointed bract (spathe); related to jack-in-the-pulpit: AR-ROW-ARUM (*Peltandra virginica*)

Figure 127

n. Flowers blue, leaves long, narrow, pointed; fruit a dry capsule: WILD IRIS or BLUE FLAG (*Iris versicolor*)   Plate VIII, No. 6

Figure 120

PLANT DESCRIPTIONS

ROSE POGONIA
or SNAKE'S-MOUTH ORCHID   *Pogonia ophioglossoides*
Figure 120

This is another of the small, fragrant orchids growing 6
to 12 inches tall with two leaves, one near the middle
of the stem, the other just under the flower. The clear
pink, infrequently white flowers are about an inch broad
and single on the stem. The spreading flower parts are
above a bearded and fringed lip.

DWARF CRANBERRY   *Vaccinium Oxycoccos*   Figure 121

This dainty little vine has pale pink, nodding flowers
with five turned-back petals and yellow flower parts
protruding from the center. The small, oval leaves,
whitened beneath, are flat, with pointed tips and curled
back margins. The berry is edible although strongly acid.

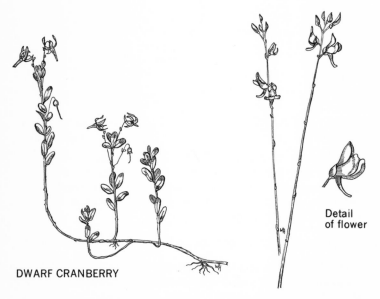

DWARF CRANBERRY

Detail
of flower

Figure 121   Figure 122

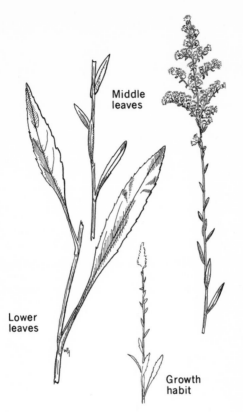

Tip
of stem

Middle
leaves

Lower
leaves

Growth
habit

Figure 123

AMERICAN CRANBERRY   *Vaccinium macrocarpon*
                                    Figure 121

This species of cranberry is somewhat similar to the preceding, but larger in every way. The leaves are pale green beneath. The edible berries are much larger and not quite so acid. This is the cranberry that is famous for its edible qualities.

HORNED BLADDERWORT *Utricularia cornuta* Figure 122

This plant often grows in masses with clusters of 3 to 6 fragrant, bright yellow, helmet-shaped flowers on 6 to 12 inch leafless stems. There is a spur, containing nectar, projecting downwards from the base of each flower.

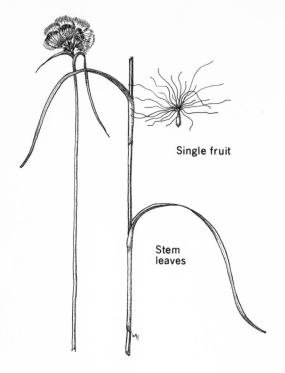

Single fruit

Stem
leaves

Figure 124

BOG GOLDENROD   *Solidago uliginosa*   Figure 123

The usually single stems of this goldenrod grow from
2½ to 4 feet high with the long leaf stems of the
toothed lower leaves clasping about half of the flower
stalk. The leaves become progressively smaller as they
ascend the stem. Flower heads are in a one-sided cluster,
slightly recurved near the tip.

COTTON-GRASS   *Eriophorum virginicum*   Figure 124

The stems of this sedge are wiry, from 1 to 2 feet tall,
with flat, long, grass-like leaves arising from the base.
This stem is surmounted by a tuft of soft, brownish-
white bristles that resemble cotton. There are two leaf-
like structures on the stem just below the cottony flower
heads.

Figure 125   Figure 126

BOGBEAN   *Menyanthes trifoliata*   Figure 125

The clusters of white, often red-tinged flowers are 5-petaled with fringes along their margins. They are borne along the upper part of the 1 to 1½ foot-tall stem. The leaves grow from a long, fleshy stem, separate from the flower stalk and are divided into three long, pointed, oval leaflets. Blooming time is late May or early June.

SWAMP AZALEA   *Rhododendron viscosum*   Figure 126

This 4 to 7 foot-tall shrub has shiny, bright green leaves which appear before the tubular, 5-lobed, very fragrant white flowers borne in clusters at the ends of the flowering branches. The buds and flower tubes are sticky.

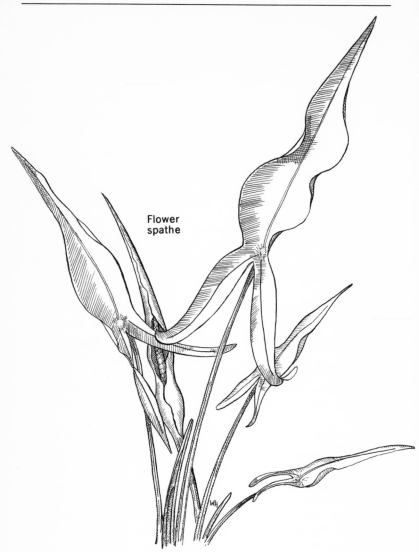

Flower
spathe

Figure 127

ARROW-ARUM   *Peltandra virginica*   Figure 127

The fleshy, broadly arrow-shaped leaves grow in a
cluster from the base. The flowers are on a central
spike shielded and nearly concealed by a green, pointed
hood which is whitish on the inside. This plant is a relative of the jack-in-the-pulpit.

PLATES

PITCHER-PLANT   *Sarracenia purpurea*   Plate VIII, No. 3

The common name well describes this unique plant. The leaves are hollow "pitchers", broadly winged, with an erect, open, bristly hood. The 4 to 6 inch long pitchers are usually partly filled with water and dead insects. The red petals, arching over a greenish-yellow center, give the flower a general circular, or disc-shaped outline. The flowers are borne singly on a leafless stem 1 to 1½ feet high. The entire plant is reddish-purple.

ARETHUSA
or SWAMP-PINK   *Arethusa bulbosa*   Plate VIII, No. 4

The flower stems of this dainty, fragrant, little orchid are 4 to 8 inches tall, rising from a bulb. The single, inconspicuous leaf sheaths and clasps the lower part of the stem. The upper parts of the single, rose-purple flower arch over a protruding lip with a yellow center.

GRASS-PINK   *Calopogon pulchellus*   Plate VIII, No. 5

This is the third and the tallest, 8 to 15 inches, of the small, pink-purple orchids. It is easily identified by the several, 1-inch broad flowers at the top of the stem. The flower parts are irregular. The lip, bearded with white, yellow, and purple hairs at the top of the flower appears hinged to the several lower, spreading floral structures.

WILD IRIS
or BLUE FLAG   *Iris versicolor*   Plate VIII, No. 6

The pale-to-bright purplish blue flowers of the "fleur-de-lis", as this plant is sometimes called, rise on stout, 1 to 2½ foot-high stems, angled on one side. The flat, sword-shaped leaves are nearly as tall as the flowering stems. The flowers are purple-veined with three drooping outer parts and three erect in the center.

CHAPTER SEVEN

FRESH WATER MARSHES
AND MEADOWS

You will find a vast array of wildflowers in the low-lying fresh water marshes that are characterized by open areas with low, dense vegetation, few or no trees, a well-developed, often mucky soil, and a plentiful supply of fresh water. The marshes usually border a stream or pond, and often grade into grass or sedge meadows. In late summer and fall, members of the Aster family are especially common. Among the impressive variety of plants found, the knotweeds (*Polygonum*) are numerous and sometimes difficult to identify. A word of caution: poison ivy and poison sumac are quite prevalent in these areas.

The slightly salty (brackish) water from tides near the mouth of fresh water streams favors a mixture of salt marsh and fresh marsh plants. Therefore, consult Chapter Four, Seashore and Salt Marshes. The key to Pond Areas, Chapter Five, may also prove helpful.

KEY TO THE WILDFLOWERS OF FRESH WATER MARSHES AND MEADOWS

a. Plants shrubby with stems more or less woody and perennial. . .b.

b. Close, bushy-branched shrubs with leafy stems and small flowers in clusters. . .c.

c. Flowers pink; clusters tall and narrow; leaves and stems reddish woolly: STEEPLE-BUSH (*Spiraea tomentosa*) Plate IX, No. 2

  c. Flowers white; clusters rounded or pyramidal; leaves and stems nearly smooth: MEADOW-SWEET (*Spiraea latifolia*) Figure 128

 b. Open-branched shrubs. . .d.

  d. Leaves compound; flowers small, white, in flat-topped clusters; leaflets narrow and deeply toothed; fruit in clusters, purple-black, edible (mostly cooked): COMMON ELDERBERRY (*Sambucus canadensis*) Plate IX, No. 3

  d. Leaves simple. . .e.

   e. Stem arching, wand-like and often rooting at tip, spongy at base; flowers purple, grouped in axils of long, narrow, whorled leaves; often extending into open water as a floating mat: WATER-WILLOW or SWAMP-LOOSESTRIFE (*Decodon verticillatus*) Chapter 5, Plate VII, No. 2

   e. Stem upright. . .f.

    f. Flowers rose-pink, large with darker center ring; leaves large, woolly beneath; blooming in late summer in colonies: ROSE-MALLOW (*Hibiscus palustris*) Chapter 4, Plate VI, No. 4

    f. Flowers white, in wispy clusters in spring; new leaves wine-red; fruit similar to blueberry but larger and seedier; juicy and sweet; medium to large shrubs or small trees: SHADBUSH or JUNEBERRY (*Amelanchier canadensis*) Plate IX, No. 4

a. Plants not shrubby, stems not woody. . .g.

 g. Flowers inconspicuous. . .h.

  h. Leaves long, narrow, reed-like. . .f.

   i. Tall plants (three feet or more in height). . .j.

    j. Leaves mostly in tussocks at base of upright stalks; fruiting clusters conspicuous as small, brown, drooping woolly balls: WOOLLY SEDGE (*Scirpus cyperinus*) Figure 129

    j. Leaves not in tussocks. . .k.

k.   Plant with conspicuous dark brown spikes at
     tips of stalk; early falling, uppermost, male
     flowers occurring without a break in the spike;
     in fruit becoming woolly: BROAD-LEAVED
     CAT-TAIL (*Typha latifolia*)   Figure 130

k.   Plant without cat-tail spikes; mid-vein of leaf
     off-center; flowers embedded in fleshy spike
     which emerges from side of leaf stalk like a
     little   finger: SWEETFLAG or CALAMUS
     (*Acorus Calamus*)   Figure 131

i.   Short plants (under 3 feet high); leaves alternate
     along flower stalk; fruit round, composed of many
     pointed nutlets: BUR-REED (*Sparganium ameri-
     canum*)   Chapter 5, Figure 104

h.   Leaves broadly arrowhead-shaped; flowers embedded
     in a white fleshy spike (spadix) surrounded by green
     (internally white), pointed bract (spathe), similar to
     Jack-in-the-pulpit: ARROW-ARUM (*Peltandra vir-
     cinica*)   Chapter 6, Figure 127

g.   Flowers conspicuous, fitting into one of the categories
     listed below:
     1. Flowers with white or greenish-white petals or
         petal-like rays.
     2. Flowers with blue, purple, or violet petals or
         petal-like rays.
     3. Flowers with red, rose, or pink petals or petal-
         like rays.
     4. Flowers with yellow or orange petals or petal-
         like rays.

1. FLOWERS WITH WHITE OR GREENISH-WHITE
    PETALS OR PETAL-LIKE RAYS

A.   Leaves compound or finely divided; flowers small, clus-
     tered, with stalks all from one point on stem (*umbel*)
     . . .B.

B.   All leaflets finely divided; umbels small; weak-stemmed
     plants often associated with brackish water: MOCK
     BISHOP'S-WEED (*Ptilimnium capillaceum*)
                                   Chapter 4, Figure 93

B.   Leaflets broadly flattened (those under water may be finely divided), coarsely toothed; umbels larger; tall, strong stemmed plants. . .C.

  C.   Stems strongly angled; mature flowering plants with upper leaflets narrow, elongate and not lobed or further divided: WATER-PARSNIP (*Sium suave*)
Figure 132

  C.   Stems not strongly angled, often purple colored at base; leaflets twice or thrice divided or lobed, broadly elongate; *Caution: plant is extremely poisonous if eaten.* SPOTTED COWBANE (*Cicuta maculata*)
Figure 133

A. Leaves simple. . .D.

  D.   Stems weak, finely prickly. . .E.

  E.   Leaves with rounded basal lobes; flowers in globular clusters, white or pink: ARROW-LEAVED TEARTHUMB (*Polygonum sagittatum*)   Figure 134

  E.   Leaves with pointed basal lobes, soft hairy beneath; flowers pink or white in elongate cluster; HALBERD-LEAVED TEARTHUMB (*Polygonum arifolium*)   Figure 134

  D.   Stems not prickly. . .F.

  F.   Flowering heads in large, flat-topped clusters; leaves opposite, long-pointed and rough hairy, often with the broad bases jointed appearing as if pierced by the upright stem: BONESET (*Eupatorium perfoliatum*)   Chapter 5, Figure 109

  F.   Flowers not in heads nor flat-topped clusters. . .G.

  G.   Flowers tiny, numerous in snowy-white, rounded or domed clusters; leaves long, narrow and whorled; stem four-angled and leaning on surrounding vegetation: WHITE BEDSTRAW (*Galium boreale*)   Figure 135

  G.   Flowers larger, leaves not whorled. . .H.

  H.   Flowers many along a short, unbranched stem; leaves toothless with parallel veins . . .I.

I.   Flowers white, spirally arranged on stem, fragrant: leaves narrowly elongate: NODDING LADIES'-TRESSES ORCHID (*Spiranthes cernua*)   Figure 136

I.   Flowers greenish-white, lower lip finely divided; leaves broadly elongate: RAGGED-FRINGED ORCHID (*Habenaria lacera*)
Plate IX, No. 5

H.   Flowers larger, white, only one occurring at the tip of each stalk; lower petal lined with purple; leaves with net-like branching from mid-vein and rounded teeth on the margin: LANCE-LEAVED VIOLET (*Viola lanceolata*)
Figure 137

2.   FLOWERS WITH BLUE, PURPLE, OR VIOLET PETAL OR PETAL-LIKE RAYS

A.   Flowers in heads with or without petal-like rays. . .B.

B.   Flowers with petal-like rays lilac or blue-violet to white; leaves long and narrow, toothless and without stalks; a tall bushy-branched plant with many flower heads the size of a quarter: NEW YORK ASTER (*Aster novi-belgii*)   Chapter 4, Figure 97

B.   Flowers without petal-like rays; heads in dome-shaped clusters, purple; leaves several at one place encircling the stem, rough-hairy; generally growing in colonies: JOE-PYE-WEED (*Eupatorium dubium*)
Plate IX, No. 6

A.   Flowers not in heads. . .C.

C.   Flowers clustered. . .D.

D.   Flowers in elongate clusters or spikes. . .E.

E.   Veins of leaf mostly parallel; leaves elongate heart-shaped; flowers above the leaves, blue-violet with yellow center; often growing in colonies in the water: PICKERELWEED (*Pontederia cordata*)   Chapter 5, Plate VII, No. 6

E.   Veins net-branched. . .F.

F.   Leaf base heart-shaped; flowers purple, with

petals free, elongate and wrinkled: SPIKED LOOSESTRIFE (*Lythrum Salicaria*)
Plate X, No. 1

F. Leaf base tapering to stalk; flowers blue or purplish; petals united at base with five rounded lobes: BLUE VERVAIN (*Verbena hastata*)
Figure 138

D. Flowers in rounded clusters, purple-brown and mauve, violet-scented; a sprawling, vine-like plant with leaves divided into five-leaflets, and edible underground tubers: GROUNDNUT or WILD BEAN (*Apios americana*)
Plate X, No. 2

C. Flowers not clustered. . .G.

G. Flowers with an upper and lower lip, blue; stem square, leaves opposite, long-oval, pointed and toothed; late summer flowering: SKULLCAP (*Scutellaria epilobiifolia*)
Figure 139

G. Flowers symmetrical. . .H.

H. Flowers larger than a half-dollar, with blue, drooping segments veined with purple; leaves large, long and grasslike: WILD IRIS or BLUE-FLAG (*Iris versicolor*) Chapter 6, Plate VIII, No. 6

H. Flowers about the size of a dime with six, blue segments, bristle-tipped; leaves narrow, grasslike; often growing in great masses in open meadows: BLUE-EYED GRASS (*Sisyrinchium angustifolium*)
Figure 140

3. FLOWERS WITH RED, ROSE, OR PINK PETALS OR PETAL-LIKE RAYS

A. Leaves compound; flowers large, five-petaled, pink. . .B.

B. Leaflets 7 or 9, coarsely toothed, oval shaped; base of compound leaf flattened and toothed: VIRGINIA ROSE (*Rosa virginiana*)   Chapter 3, Plate V, No. 3

B. Leaflets 7, finely toothed, narrowly elongate; base of compound leaf narrowly flattened, *not toothed*, otherwise like Virginia rose: SWAMP ROSE (*Rosa palustris*)   Chapter 3, Plate V, No. 3

A.   Leaves simple. . .C.

   C.   Leaves oppositely arranged, oblong, dull green, whitish beneath, flowers five petaled, pink, in a few flowered clusters; stem and leaves purple-stained in autumn: MARSH ST. JOHN'S-WORT (*Hypericum virginicum*)   Chapter 5, Figure 117

   C.   Leaves alternately arranged. . .D.

      D.   Leaves elongate, pointed at both ends; flowers drooping, densely clustered at top of stalk, bright pink: PINKWEED (*Polygonum pensylvanicum*) and the slightly varied LADY'S THUMB (*Polygonum Persicaria*)   Chapter 3, Figure 69

4.   FLOWERS WITH YELLOW OR ORANGE PETALS OR PETAL-LIKE RAYS

A.   Flowers in small, densely clustered yellow-orange heads, petal-like rays inconspicuous in the mass; leaves rough-hairy. . .B.

   B.   Leaves long, narrow and pointed with three main veins, margin sharply toothed; clusters drooping at tips or recurved: CANADA GOLDENROD (*Solidago canadensis*)   Figure 141

   B.   Leaves broadly elongate, with one main vein and numerous branches; clusters light yellow, with upright, rough-hairy branches: ROUGH-STEMMED GOLDENROD (*Solidago rugosa*)   Figure 142

A.   Flowers not in clustered heads. . .C.

   C.   Flowers large, drooping, petals orange-yellow with brown spots; leaves narrow and pointed, alternate or whorled along the tall (3 to 7 feet) stem: TURK'S-CAP-LILY (*Lilium superbum*)   Plate X, No. 3

   C.   Flowers smaller. . .D.

      D.   Flowers orange, tubular with a curved, hollow spur; leaves alternate, light green; when seed capsules ripen, explosive on contact: JEWELWEED or TOUCH-ME-NOT (*Impatiens pallida*)
                                   Plate X, No. 4

D. Flowers in an upright spike with 5 separate yellow petals with darker lines; leaves opposite, pointed at both ends: SWAMP-CANDLES (*Lysimachia terrestris*) Plate X, No. 5

Tip
of stem

Growth
habit

Figure 128

PLANT DESCRIPTIONS

MEADOW-SWEET   *Spiraea latifolia*   Figure 128

The many, leafy stems, 2½ to 3½ feet high, are nearly smooth. The leaves do not have the whitish wool on the under surface that is found on the steeple-bush. The loose, pyramidal cluster of white flowers is at the top of the stem.

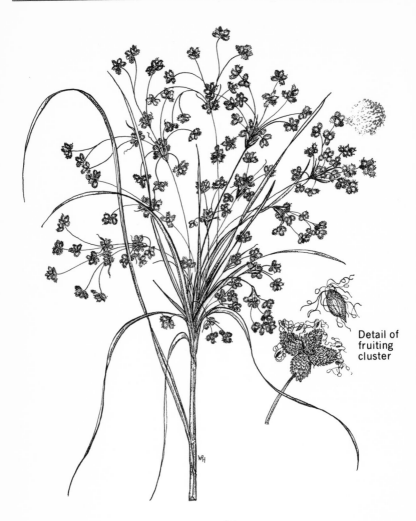

Detail of
fruiting
cluster

Figure 129

WOOLLY SEDGE   *Scirpus cyperinus*   Figure 129

This sedge grows 3 to 4 feet tall and is quite conspicuous in early fall with its many-branched fruiting clusters
consisting of brown, woolly balls in closely packed
bunches of 6 to 12 at the ends of the somewhat drooping, slender branchlets. The leaves are long and narrow,
in clumps, with the tall, stiff-flowering stems rising a-
bove them.

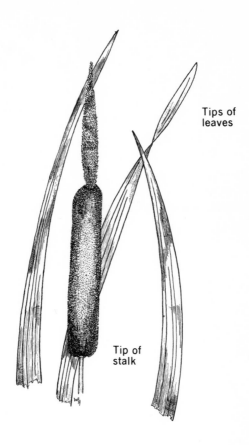

Tips of
leaves

Tip of
stalk

Figure 130

BROAD-LEAVED CAT-TAIL   *Typha latifolia*
                                        Figure 130

The long, sword-like, waving leaves of the cat-tails have
tall flowering stems rising 5 to 6 feet above them, each
with a cylindrical, brush-like cluster of dark brown
flowers. These flowers are followed by a rounded spike
which soon breaks open into a fluffy mass of down attached to the seeds.

Spadix

Figure 131

SWEETFLAG
or CALAMUS   *Acorus Calamus*   Figure 131

The leaves are similar to those of the cat-tails, except
that the mid-vein is off center, and the plant does not
have the distinctive "cat-tail". The flowers are in the
fleshy spike which protrudes from the leaf stalk.

WATER-PARSNIP   *Sium suave*   Figure 132

The stout, hollow, angled stem with its disk-shaped
cluster of white flowers, rises 2 to 4 feet high. The
leaves at the base are much divided into narrow, sharp-
ly-toothed leaflets with long leaf stems clasping the
flowering stalk. The upper leaves are not as much
divided; those at the top are without divisions.

Figure 132

SPOTTED COWBANE   *Cicuta maculata*   Figure 133

Beware of this plant; all parts are deadly poisonous if eaten. The characteristically purple-streaked stem is not angled. The leaves are two or three times divided into coarsely toothed leaflets. The disk of white flowers is more open and loosely arranged than in other similar flowers and the stems of each individual floweret are unequal.

Figure 133

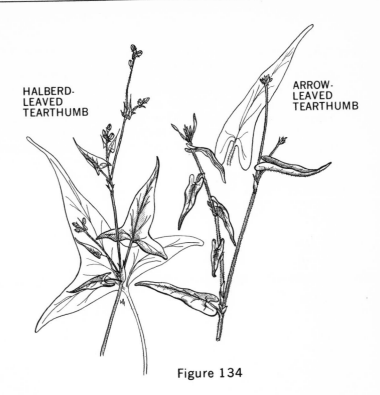

HALBERD-
LEAVED
TEARTHUMB

ARROW-
LEAVED
TEARTHUMB

Figure 134

ARROW-LEAVED TEARTHUMB   *Polygonum sagittatum*
Figure 134

The 4-angled stem, the leaf stems, and the veins of the
leaves on the under side are armed with recurving
prickles sharp enough to cut the flesh. The plant may be
found reclining, erect, or even climbing with its very
sharp prickles. The pink or white flowers are in small,
tightly packed clusters at the ends of smooth stems.
Leaves are tapering, with an arrow-shaped base.

HALBERD-LEAVED TEARTHUMB   *Polygonum arifolium*
Figure 134

Also prickly with broadly tapering leaves, not arrow-
shaped, but with two lobes projecting outward at the
base. The leaf stems on this species are relatively longer
than the preceding one. Flowers are arranged along the
ends of the stems, rather than in tight clusters, and are
pink or white.

Figure 135

WHITE BEDSTRAW   *Galium boreale*   Figure 135

The weak, slender stem reclines against neighboring
plants. The leaves are narrow, lance-shaped and arranged
in whorls of four around the square stem. The tiny,
white flowers are numerous in clusters at the ends of
the stems.

NODDING LADIES'-TRESSES ORCHID   *Spiranthes cernua*
                                        Figure 136

The slender, spirally twisted flower stalks of this dainty
little orchid rise 6 to 12 inches with several long, narrow
leaves at the base of the stem; there are a few much
smaller, clasping leaves on the upper portion beneath
the flower spike. The flowers are fragrant, somewhat
down-tilted, with a wavy lip.

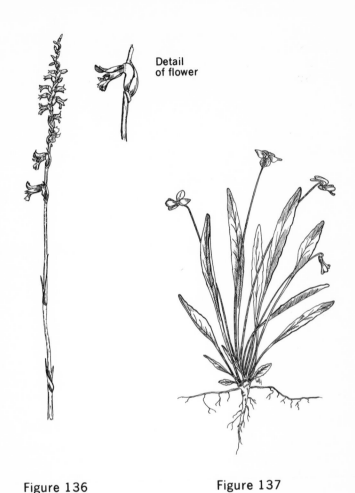

Detail of flower

Figure 136

Figure 137

LANCE-LEAVED VIOLET *Viola lanceolata* Figure 137

This entire plant is smooth with the spring leaves lance-shaped, with rounded teeth, about three times as long as wide; later leaves are larger, often as much as 4 to 6 inches long. All grow from a clump directly above the rootstock. Flowers, borne singly on the slender stems, are white with a purple-veined lip and rise 3 to 6 inches.

BLUE VERVAIN   *Verbena hastata*   Figure 138

This 3 to 4 foot-high plant with 4-sided, roughish stems has opposite, narrowly oval leaves. Flower stalks grow from the point where the upper leaves and main stem meet. The blue flowers are in short spikes at the top of the plant or its side branches.

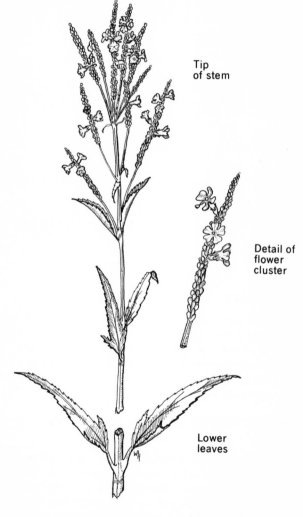

Tip
of stem

Detail of
flower
cluster

Lower
leaves

Figure 138

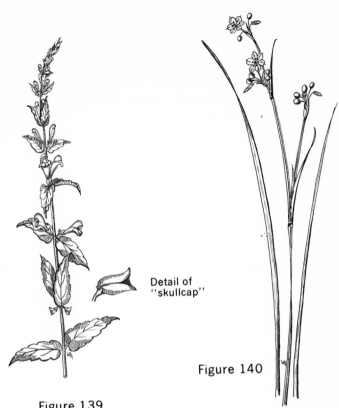

Detail of
"skullcap"

Figure 140

Figure 139

SKULLCAP   *Scutellaria epilobiifolia*   Figure 139

The 4-angled stem is 8 to 15 inches tall with soft hairs along the angles. The upper part of the plant has many branches arising from the point where the opposite, lance-shaped leaves join the main stem. The small blue flowers have two lips, the upper arched, the lower spreading with a tiny notch at the tip.

BLUE-EYED GRASS   *Sisyrinchium angustifolium*
Figure 140

This plant, growing 6 to 12 inches tall among the grasses of the moist meadows, is inconspicuous until its bright blue flowers appear. The leaves are grass-like, with parallel veins. The 6-parted flowers have a tiny bristle at the tip of each of the segments.

CANADA GOLDENROD   *Solidago canadensis*   Figure 141

This 3 to 4 foot-high goldenrod has several characteristics that distinguish it from the rough-stemmed goldenrod. The leaves are narrower and smooth to the touch, not wrinkled, and with three distinct main veins. The flower clusters are large and dense with flower heads close together; the general outline is broadly pyramidal, with the tips somewhat recurved.

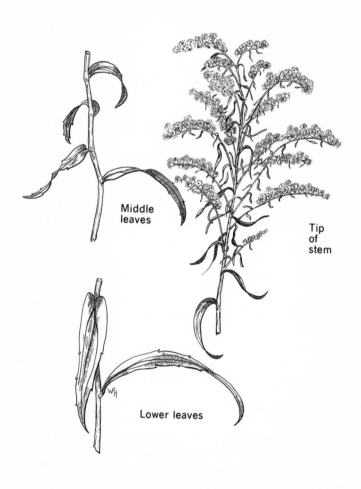

Figure 141

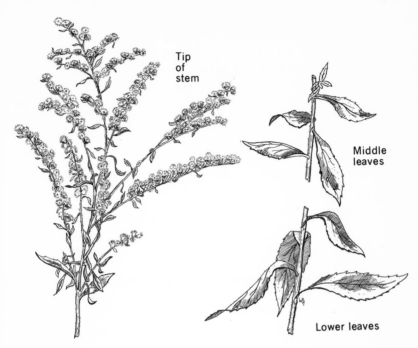

Tip
of
stem

Middle
leaves

Lower leaves

Figure 142

ROUGH-STEMMED GOLDENROD   *Solidago rugosa*
                                            Figure 142

This goldenrod often covers large areas with its crowded 3 to 4 foot-high plants. Its distinctive features include rough, wrinkled leaves with one main vein, many side branches, and a flower cluster varying from narrowly compact to open, broadly spreading and branched.

PLATES

STEEPLE-BUSH   *Spiraea tomentosa*   Plate IX, No. 2

A shrub, 3 to 4 feet tall, with very fuzzy stems and leaves. The alternate, oval leaves are toothed, dull green above and greenish-to-whitish green beneath. The "steeple" of pink flowers is at the top of the stem. It is commonly found with its close relative the meadow-sweet, from which it can be distinguished by its pink flowers. Both plants bloom from late July to mid-August.

COMMON ELDERBERRY   *Sambucus canadensis*
                                            Plate IX, No. 3

This tall shrub grows 5 or more feet tall in large
clumps. Leaves are compound with 5 to 11 leaflets.
White flowers are in large, flat clusters, followed by
purple-black, berry-like fruits which are sometimes used
in making elderberry wine. The Latin name is from an
ancient Greek musical instrument, *sambuce;* the woody
stems have a large central pith which can be punched
out leaving a hollow tube for making flutes and whistles.

SHADBUSH
or JUNEBERRY   *Amelanchier canadensis*   Plate IX, No. 4

The spring floral display of these tall shrubs (or small
trees) growing to 20 feet high, is rivaled only by the
beach-plums. The leaves appear a few days before the
blossoms and are bronzy-red. The large, showy, white
flowers are in loose clusters which tend to droop. An
edible, bluish-black fruit follows.

RAGGED FRINGED-ORCHID   *Habenaria lacera*
                                            Plate IX, No. 5

The spike of greenish-white flowers is 10 to 15 inches
tall, with the oblong lance-shaped leaves clasping the
stem and becoming progressively smaller as they ap-
proach the flower spike. All have parallel veins, a
characteristic of all the orchids. The flower lip is deeply
cut into three parts, each heavily fringed.

JOE-PYE-WEED   *Eupatorium dubium*   Plate IX, No. 6

Masses of this stout-stemmed, rank-growing plant color
the meadows with clusters of rose-purple flowers at the
top of the 3 to 4 foot-high stems. The large, oval leaves,
3 to 5 at the same point on the stem are rough and
veiny with toothed margins.

SPIKED LOOSESTRIFE   *Lythrum Salicaria*   Plate X, No. 1

This coarse-growing plant, 3 to 4½ feet tall, soon chokes
out other forms of lower vegetation and establishes itself
in large colonies. The lance-shaped leaves opposite or in
whorls of three, with a heart-shaped, or clasping, base
are without stems. The showy, magenta flowers are in
long, dense terminal spikes.

GROUNDNUT
or WILD BEAN   *Apios americana*   Plate X, No. 2

This slender vine climbs over neighboring bushes to a
height of 6 feet or more. The leaves are compound, with
3 to 5 leaflets. The edible rootstock consists of small
tubers strung together like a necklace. The purplish-
brown and mauve flowers, shaped like a small sweet
pea, are in terminal clusters.

TURK'S-CAP-LILY   *Lilium superbum*   Plate X, No. 3

The stout stems of this gorgeous lily are 3 to 7 feet
tall, with whorls of narrow, pointed leaves. The upper
leaves are sometimes alternate, not whorled. The large,
brilliant, purple-brown spotted, orange-yellow flowers
bloom in a loose pyramid in mid-August, sometimes
forming groups of 12 to 20 on a single stalk with the
lowest bud opening first. The six strongly recurved segments of the drooping flowers give it the "turk's-cap"
appearance.

JEWELWEED
or TOUCH-ME-NOT   *Impatiens pallida*   Plate X, No. 4

This 2 to 4 foot-high plant usually grows in colonies.
The alternate leaves are oval and coarsely toothed; they
have a silvery appearance when placed under water.
The tubular flowers with flaring petals and a curved,
hollow spur hang suspended from near the middle by a
slender stem. The fat, oval, green seed pods burst dis-
concertingly when touched and eject the seeds a considerable distance.

SWAMP-CANDLES   *Lysimachia terrestris*   Plate X, No. 5

This very leafy, loosely-branched plant is 15 to 30 inches
tall with opposite leaves pointed at both ends. The dark
lined, 5-petaled, yellow, star-like flowers are on slender
stems ascending to make a loose, upright spike.

CHAPTER EIGHT

SWAMPLANDS

Swampland plants inhabit moist areas that are frequently flooded or located near bodies of water and are covered by tall shrubs and shading trees. Although there are several types of swamplands on Cape Cod, the wildflowers found in them do not vary greatly. The dense, acid, watery stands of the Atlantic White Cedar swamplands are more intriguing in themselves than they are productive of wildflowers. On the other hand, in the spring, before leaves appear on the trees, masses of wildflowers bloom in the red maple and tupelo swamplands. By autumn, the foliage reaches a hot intensity of red, scarlet, golden-orange and purple.

Shrubby swamplands are hard to explore and have few conspicuous flowers except for the shrubs themselves, but they often contain the biggest and juiciest high-bush blueberries and juneberries. If you are lucky enough to spend a whole summer near the shrubby swamplands, you will revel in the progression of whiteness. First in early spring, the shad bush or juneberry blooms wispy white, with wine-red new leaves. In June follow the flat-topped clusters of small, red-centered, white flowers of the black chokeberry (not choke-cherry). Early July finds the swamp azalea in full, fragrant bloom; the reddish, sticky, outer surface of the flowers protecting them from pollen-pirating ants who would threaten seed formation by leaving nothing to pollinate the flowers. And as a final wave to summer in late August, the sweet pepperbush lights the swamplands with its white, sweetly-scented, candle-like flower clusters.

Go forth with a feeling of adventure and not with fear to the swamplands, where boots might be an advantage, mosquito repellent might save you from slight distractions, and long-sleeved shirts and long trousers might keep you from knowing the catbrier too intimately. The rare snake or spider found in Cape swamps is completely harmless.

KEY TO WILDFLOWERS OF THE SWAMPLANDS

a. Plants vine-like or shrubby. . .b.

  b. Plants vine-like, either high climbers or running along the ground. . .c.

    c. Plants thorny, leaves simple, rounded; stems with stout prickles and grasping tendrils; flowers inconspicuous, bell-shaped, dull yellow-green; fruit a cluster of blue-black berries. . .d.

      d. Lower surface of leaves bluish-green, powdery; leaves broadly oval, sometimes pointed and with mottling on the surface: CATBRIER (*Smilax glauca*) Figure 143

      d. Lower surface of leaves green, shiny; leaves rounded, not mottled: BULLBRIER (*Smilax rotundifolia*) Figure 143

    c. Plants not thorny; leaves compound, divided into three, shiny leaflets, the middle one the largest; flower inconspicuous; fruit clusters of creamy-white papery-skinned nutlets: POISON IVY (*Rhus radicans*) Chapter 3, Figure 36

  b. Plants shrubby. . .e.

    e. Flowers conspicuous. . .f.

      f. Flowers very fragrant. . .g.

        g. Flowers large, reddish sticky outside and in bud; leaves small, dark green, shiny, turning purplish in autumn: SWAMP AZALEA (*Rhododendron viscosum*) Chapter 6, Figure 126

        g. Flowers small, but clustered in upright spikes; leaves long oval, broadest near the toothed tip: SWEET PEPPERBUSH (*Clethra alnifolia*) Plate XI, No. 1

      f. Flowers not especially fragrant, blooming in spring; sometimes reaching small tree size; fruit similar to blueberry but larger, seedy but sweet and edible, often neglected: SHADBUSH or JUNEBERRY (*Amelanchier canadensis*) Chapter 7, Plate IX, No. 4

    e. Flowers inconspicuous; leaves compound, divided into 7-13 pairs of smooth, elongate, pointed leaflets; fruit in hanging clusters, ivory-white nutlets; foliage orange or scarlet in autumn: POISON SUMAC (*Rhus vernix*)   Chapter 3, Figure 36

a. Plants not vine-like or shrubby. . .h.

  h. Flowers inserted on a fleshy spike (spadix) covered and hooded by a purple-mottled bract (spathe); leaves divided into three parts, fruit a cluster of scarlet berries: JACK-IN-THE-PULPIT (*Arisaema triphyllum*)   Plate XI, No. 2

  h. Flowers not as above. . .i.

    i. Flowers white. . .j.

      j. Flowers star-shaped on delicate stalks; leaves whorled, long and pointed; fruit tiny white capsules: STAR-FLOWER or MAYSTAR (*Trientalis borealis*)   Chapter 1, Figure 8

      j. Flowers not star-shaped. . .k.

        k. Flowers tiny and clustered along a short spike; leaves oval, usually only two fruit, a ruby-red berry: CANADA MAYFLOWER or WILD LILY-OF-THE-VALLEY (*Maianthemum canadense*)   Chapter 1, Figure 7

        k. Flowers larger, not clustered. . .l.

          l. Leaves compound. . .m.

            m. Summer blooming, prickly-stemmed bramble with drooping 5-petaled flowers in small clusters and a red, rounded, warty fruit which falls thimble-shaped from the bush when ripe; leaflets gray or white beneath: RED RASPBERRY (*Rubus species*)   Chapter 2, Figure 24

            m. Spring blooming, low, herbaceous plants usually growing in large colonies; leaves divided into 3 to 5 soft green leaflets; flowers often pink-tinged outside: WOOD-ANEMONE (*Anemone quinquefolia*)   Figure 144

    l. Leaves simple, rounded. . .n.

        n. Flowers single on a stalk from root-crown; lower petal purple streaked; fruit a 3-parted capsule: PALE VIOLET (*Viola pallens*)   Figure 145

        n. Flowers several along a stalk, nodding; leaves several from the root-crown, shiny: SHINLEAF (*Pyrola elliptica*)   Chapter 1, Figure 3

  i. Flowers red, with a white-fringed tip extending above the lower lip; tall plant with long, toothed, pointed leaves: CARDINAL-FLOWER (*Lobelia Cardinalis*)   Plate XI, No. 3

PLANT DESCRIPTIONS

CATBRIER   *Smilax glauca*   Figure 143

This vine, together with the following species, forms almost impenetrable thickets as it climbs over neighboring shrubs. The green stem is armed with numerous sharp prickles. The leaves are broadly oval, narrowing toward the more or less pointed tip; they are a lighter, bluish-green beneath and may appear powdery. Coiled tendrils serve for climbing. Small, yellowish-green, 6-petaled flowers are in rounded clusters where leaves and climbing stem join; these are followed by bluish-black berries.

BULLBRIER   *Smilax rotundifolia*   Figure 143

The bullbrier is stouter than the preceding vine, and has many 4-angled branches. The prickles are heavier, although not as numerous. The rounded leaves are shiny green, not lighter beneath and without the mottling that sometimes appears on the catbrier. Flowers are similar to the above, but the bluish-black berries are covered with a bloom.

WOOD-ANEMONE   *Anemone quinquefolia*   Figure 144

This little plant, 4 to 8 inches tall, has three long-stemmed, compound leaves, each with five leaflets, growing from the same point at the top of the slender, wiry stem. The single, 5-petaled, white flower, frequently with faint pink or purple markings on the under surface, is borne on a stem that arises from the same point as the leaf stems. Many of the swamps, particularly the Seashore's red maple swamp in Eastham, are carpeted with the dainty flowers in mid-May.

PALE VIOLET   *Viola pallens*   Figure 145

This small, white violet with brownish-purple veins on the lower petals, grows 3 to 5 inches tall with the flower stems overtopping the leaves. The broadly oval leaves have rounded tips and heart-shaped bases.

PLATES

SWEET PEPPERBUSH   *Clethra alnifolia*   Plate XI, No. 1

This shrub, 3 to 8 feet tall, is white with fragrant bloom from mid-to-late August. The erect spikes of small, clustered white blossoms are very attractive to bees, small moths and butterflies. The toothed leaves are a lengthened oval, much broader at the tips.

JACK-IN-THE-PULPIT   *Arisaema triphyllum*
                                        Plate XI, No. 2

This stout, erect plant grows 1 to 2½ feet high, usually with two large leaves composed of three oval, toothless, pointed leaflets. The central, fleshy flower spike (the "jack") is enclosed in a tubular, vase-like structure (the "pulpit") with an overhanging hood. The "pulpit" varies in color from light green to dark green heavily striped with purplish-brown. The fruit is a cluster of bright, orange-red berries.

CARDINAL-FLOWER   *Lobelia Cardinalis* Plate XI, No. 3

The long spike of this stout-stemmed, pure red flower grows 1½ to 3 feet tall and is quickly identified by its brilliant color. The leaves are broadly lance-shaped, toothed, with pointed tips.

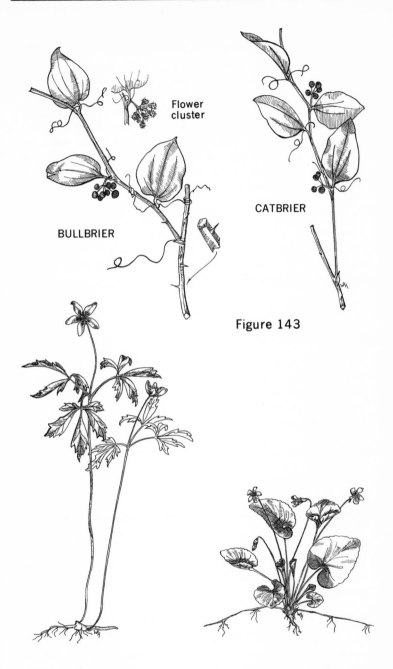

Flower cluster

BULLBRIER

CATBRIER

Figure 143

Figure 144

Figure 145

BIBLIOGRAPHY

All nomenclature used in this book has been conformed to *Gray's New Manual of Botany,* 8th edition. The following books are recommended to the reader who wishes to explore further into the world of wild plants:

GENERAL

Dana, Mrs. William S. *How to Know the Wild Flowers,* revised by Clarence J. Hylander. New York: Dover Publications, 1963.

Hylander, Clarence J. *Flowers of Field and Forest.* New York: The Macmillan Co., 1962.

Lemmon, Robert S. and Charles C. Johnson *Wildflowers of North America in Full Color.* Garden City: Hanover House, 1961.

Mathews, F. Schuyler. *A Field Book of American Wild Flowers.* New York: G. P. Putnam's Sons.

Petry, Dr. Loren C. *A Beachcomber's Botany,* Illustrated by Marcia Gaylord Norman (revised ed. of *Treasures of the Shore*) Chatham, Mass.: The Chatham Conservation Foundation, Inc. 1968.

Rickett, Harold W. *The New Field Book of American Wild Flowers.* New York: G. P. Putnam's Sons, 1963.

Rickett, H. W. *Wildflowers of the United States, Vol. 1, The Northeastern States.* New York: The McGraw-Hill Book Co., 1966.

Stupka, Arthur. *Wildflowers in Color.* New York: Harper & Row, 1965.

Wherry, Dr. Edgar T. *Wild Flower Guide.* New York: Doubleday & Co., 1948.

WILDFLOWER CULTIVATION

Coon, Nelson. *Using Wayside Plants.* New York: The Hearthside Press, 1960.

Hershey, Jean. *Wild Flowers to Know and Grow.* New York: The Van Nostrand Co., 1964.

Taylor, Kathryn S. and Stephen F. Hamblin *Handbook of Wild Flower Cultivation.* New York: The Macmillan Co., 1962.

REFERENCE WORKS

Britton, N. L. and Brown, A. *Illustrated Flora of the Northeastern United States and Adjacent Canada,* 3 vols., revised by H. A. Gleason. New York: Hafner Publishing Co., 1947.

Robinson, B. L. and M. L. Fernald. *Gray's New Manual of Botany,* 8th edition. New York: The American Book Co., 1947.

INDEX

Wildflowers of Cape Cod

WILDFLOWERS
of CAPE COD

by
HAROLD R. HINDS &
WILFRED A. HATHAWAY

Photographs by the Authors

Pen and Ink Drawings by
WILFRED A. HATHAWAY

THE CHATHAM PRESS, INC., CHATHAM, MASS.

ACKNOWLEDGMENTS

Many have been of assistance in the inspiration and preparation of this volume, not the least of whom are those questioning people who have asked the naturalists of the National Seashore, "Where can we find a guide to help us with the flowers in this area?"

Sincere acknowledgement is extended to the Department of the Interior personnel of the Cape Cod National Seashore, especially to the first Chief Naturalist of the park, Vernon S. (Tommy) Gilbert, who made the initial suggestion for the writing of such a guide; to his successor, Earl Estes, who laid the groundwork for its publication; and to the present Chief Naturalist, Vernon D. Dame, who helped it to fruition.

We would like to thank Robert Taylor, Clark L. Thayer, John Burk and Robert Boles for their expert advice.

We are indebted to our wives, Judy Hinds and Marion Hathaway, for their cooperation and forbearance throughout the vicissitudes that occurred during the preparation of the material for this book.

Harold R. Hinds
Wilfred A. Hathaway
January, 1968

INTRODUCTION

Today, with automobiles to transport us from one location to another, wildflowers tend to become a blur of colors as we rush past fields and roadsides. We take them for granted as simply being there. Yet, these flowers, which are only one element in the make-up and life of a plant, can become a fascinating and relaxing hobby. It is a pursuit that can lead (on bright days) to remote and beautiful parts of the woods, fields or dunes in search of new specimens; while in poor weather, you can relax with a flower book or magazine, seeking more knowledge of plants you have found or descriptions of those you will seek on your next walk.

In order to separate one type of flower from all others or recognize another of the same kind, it is important to have a name for the plant. Thus, the first purpose of this, as well as most other field guides, is to enable you to answer the question, "What is it?" Secondly, and almost equally important, is the relationship your specimen bears to others of its species and habitat. As you progress in your study of wildflowers, the plants around you will fall into well-organized patterns, each having its own special characteristics within an orderly system.

Over 600 plant specimens have been recorded on Cape Cod. Two-thirds of these, however, are found only in isolated areas, or widely scattered among the common plants. The other third, or some 200 species, are common not only to the Cape, but for the most part to the coastal plains of New England. It is with these species that *Wildflowers of Cape Cod* is principally concerned.

Plants included in this book have been listed in four ways: by keys; by plant descriptions; visually by drawings and color photos; and alphabetically in the index. Since the majority of plants is confined to certain areas where conditions are suited to their particular growing requirements, we have grouped them according to the place, or *habitat*, where they are most commonly found. The boundaries of these habitats merge into one another, and some plants have adapted themselves to two or more habitats. For that reason, you will find a few plants keyed in more than one chapter.

IDENTIFYING YOUR PLANT

If you are using a flower guide for the first time, you will undoubtedly take a quick glance at the keys and decide that they are not for the amateur. On the contrary, while keys may appear complicated at first, they are fun to use, and can be easily mastered with a little practice and patience.

The first step to identification by keys is an understanding of the terms used to describe plants. Imagine that you have discovered some unknown wild plant, and are observing it in its native habitat.

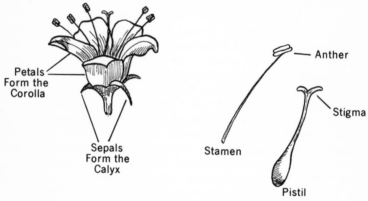

PARTS OF A FLOWER

Perhaps, first of all, you will notice its flowers. Look closely at a new flower to decide whether it is a single flower with numerous parts, or whether it is composed of many, tiny, individual flowers. Diagram 1 shows the principal parts — petals, sepals, stamens and pistils — which together constitute a single *flower*, as in the familiar rose or buttercup. Many blossoms that at first appear to be a single flower are members of the *Composite* family which have many, tiny flowers. Each tiny flower is composed of the principal parts mentioned above, and are massed into a *head*. Plants of this large family on Cape Cod include, among others, the aster, goldenrod, daisy, dandelion, sunflower and black-eyed Susan.

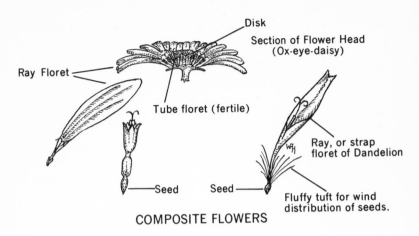

COMPOSITE FLOWERS

There are three general types of composites. First, in the daisy, (Plate IV, No. 5) you can observe many tiny flowers packed closely together in one head. Also in this category are the goldenrod and others which have their tiny flowers grouped into many heads. The outer "petals" of these flowers, called *rays*, are one-sided female flowers, while the inner yellow disk is composed of many, tightly packed, tubular flowers with both male and female parts.

The second and third types of composite are those flowers which have heads composed only of rays or only of disks. One common example of the ray type is the dandelion (Page 59) with its tubular flowers each having a strap-shaped, one-sided extension. The common tansy (Page 53) is typical of the disk type.

Having decided whether your flower is single, or one of the three composite types, you should next consider whether it is *conspicuous* or *inconspicuous*. These terms are fairly obvious, and are used to differentiate plants with easily noticed flowers from those such as grasses, sedges and some ocean-side plants whose foliage is more distinctive than their flowers.

Next, observe the form of the leaves. If there are two at each portion on the stem, they are *opposite*. If you see only one leaf at each position, the pattern is called *alternate*. When the arrangement is *whorled*, several leaves surround the stem at each position. Leaves are *compound* when each one is divided into smaller leaves or leaflets. Study the diagrams that follow and compare them to leaves of plants in your yard or nearby fields.

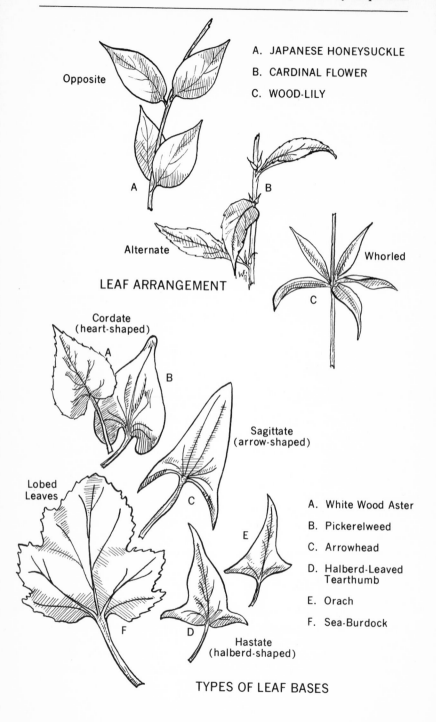

Opposite

A. JAPANESE HONEYSUCKLE
B. CARDINAL FLOWER
C. WOOD-LILY

A

B

Alternate

Whorled

C

LEAF ARRANGEMENT

Cordate
(heart-shaped)

A

B

Sagittate
(arrow-shaped)

Lobed
Leaves

C

E

A. White Wood Aster

B. Pickerelweed

C. Arrowhead

D. Halberd-Leaved
Tearthumb

E. Orach

F. Sea-Burdock

F

D

Hastate
(halberd-shaped)

TYPES OF LEAF BASES

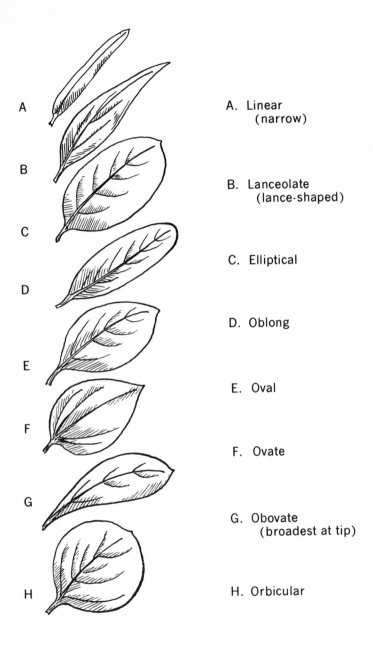

A. Linear
   (narrow)

B. Lanceolate
   (lance-shaped)

C. Elliptical

D. Oblong

E. Oval

F. Ovate

G. Obovate
   (broadest at tip)

H. Orbicular

LEAF SHAPES

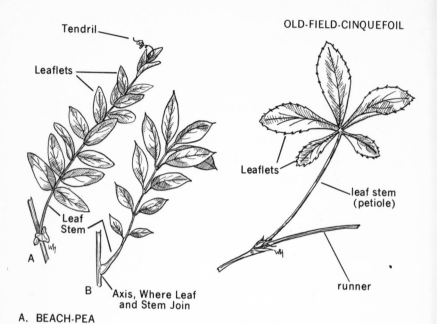

OLD-FIELD-CINQUEFOIL

Tendril

Leaflets

Leaflets

leaf stem
(petiole)

Leaf
Stem

A

B   Axis, Where Leaf
    and Stem Join

runner

A. BEACH-PEA
B. POISON SUMAC   PALMATELY
                        COMPOUND LEAF

Botanists distinguish some plants from others by the kind of *fruit* they bear. The term fruit does not necessarily indicate a fleshy growth, but refers to all types of seed containers such as capsules, berries, grains, nutlets, pomes (apple or apple-like fruits), and drupes (cherry-like fruits).

Before identifying some plants with certainty, you will need to examine their stems. The alternatives, *shrubby,* and *not shrubby* or *herbaceous,* serve to distinguish between two fairly obvious categories of plants. A shrubby plant has woody stems and does not die back to the ground each winter. Because these plants also live for more than three years, they are called *perennials.* On the other hand, an herbaceous plant or herb has no woody stem. It may live for one growing season (an *annual*); for two (a *biennial*); or it may be a perennial. *Herbaceous perennials* die back to the ground each winter, but underground stems remain alive in several forms: buds on the top of a root crown, bulbs, corms, or tubers. A *succulent* plant is one in which the stem and/or leaves are thick, fleshy and watery. Many of the seashore and salt marsh plants have this characteristic.

HOW TO USE THE KEYS

Once you have mastered the basic terms, you are ready to follow a key to its destination — the identification of your particular plant.

The secret to keys is the ability to differentiate between the observed features of your specimen and the *opposite* of those features.

The simplest example is found in the Key to Habitats following this Introduction. In this key, the first letter A indicates Uplands; the second A several lines down is Lowlands. You must be in one or the other place; it is impossible to be in both places at one time. Thus, you make your choice between the first and second A. If you are in Uplands, move to the next letter B. The area around you is either wooded or open. If it is wooded, you have reached your goal — Chapter One. If it is open, you still have two choices; recently disturbed areas or areas of low heath. By selecting the proper C, you decide upon Chapter Three or Chapter Two.

The same principal of narrowing your choice by selecting one of two opposites applies in greater depth to the plant keys themselves. By tracing the following example through to its conclusion, you will find how easy it can be to identify plants by keys.

Suppose that you have chosen the Seashore and Salt Marsh Habitat, Chapter Four, from the habitat key. Turning to page 82, you decide first of all that your plant is *not shrubby*. Therefore, you disregard the first a. and all of the entries beneath it, thumbing down until you find the second a. on page 83. You then select the first g., because the flowers are inconspicuous rather than conspicuous; the second h. because the leaves are unlobed rather than lobed.

Making similar choices, you proceed through the second j., the second m., to the first n., which you choose because the stems are lying flat on the sand. At this point, you will make some additional observations. If you notice a sheath at the base of the leaf, encircling the stem, you need go no further in the key; you have identified the plant as the SEABEACH-KNOTWEED, named under the first o. as Figure 83. As a final check, turn to figure 83 and compare your specimen with the drawing and descriptive text.

Always read through both choices to decide which is most appropriate. If your result appears to be in error, check back to be certain you have correctly analyzed the characteristics of the plant, and that you are in the right habitat. Then, work through the key again. After a very few tries you will find yourself running smoothly through them each time.

One final word of caution: before starting on your first self-guided field exploration, learn to recognize three common plants. These are poison ivy and poison sumac (Figure 36), and spotted cowbane (Figure 133). Contact with the first two can cause severe skin irritation; the third is deadly poisonous if chewed or eaten. Recognizing these poisonous plants on sight can save you considerable distress, and will allow you to enjoy all the other *Wildflowers of Cape Cod.*

KEY TO HABITATS AND CHAPTERS

A. Uplands (areas with relatively dry soil, not influenced by nearness of water). . .B.

   B. Wooded areas of scrubby or large trees and their dry borders (see Chapter Two for heathland plants straying into open woods):   Chapter One, WOODLANDS

   B. Open areas. . .C.

      C. Areas of recent disturbance by man such as roadsides, lawns, waste areas, old house sites, fields overgrown with red cedar, or cleared and scraped areas:
Chapter Three, DISTURBED AREAS

      C. Areas of low heath or heather-like aspect with close, low-growing shrubs and herbs scattered throughout; low trees common but widely spaced; often extending to sandy borders of woodlands (see Chapter One, above), road embankments and dunes; flowers mostly of spring and summer blooming (see Chapter Six for boggy dune hollows):
Chapter Two, HEATHLANDS AND DUNES

A. Lowlands (area of open water or moist soil, open or shaded) . . .D.

   D. Open areas without trees. . .E.

      E. Areas influenced by the sea and tides, either the sea beach with loose sand, or tidal marshes with richer, darker soil and grassy borders: Chapter Four, SEASHORE AND
SALT MARSHES

E.   Areas influenced by fresh water, moist soil, springs, ponds and streams. . .F.

   F.   Open bodies of water and the **immediate** shore (see Chapter Four for salt pond vegetation):
                       Chapter Five, POND AREAS

   F.   Moist or wet lowlands often surrounding open bodies of water. . .G.

     G.   Lowland areas of present or former cranberry cultivation; moist, sandy, between-dune areas; or quaking, mossy or low shrubby areas or borders of muddy ponds with little or no drainage; flowers mostly of spring and early summer: Chapter Six, BOGLANDS

     G.   Open bushy (not tall shrubby) or grassy lowlands often bordering streams; flowers mostly of summer and fall: Chapter Seven, FRESH MARSHES AND MEADOWS

D.   Shaded lowland areas with tall shrubs and trees; with or without open water; flowers mostly spring blooming:
                       Chapter Eight, SWAMPLANDS

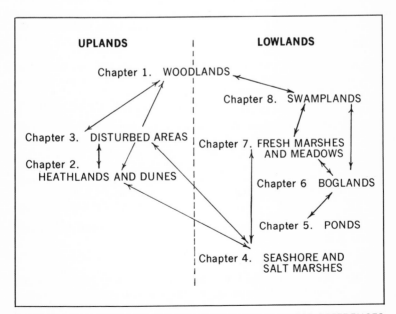

DIAGRAM OF HABITAT INTERGRADATIONS AND CHAPTER REFERENCES

THE MAYFLOWER

In the gleam and gloom of the April weather,
    When the snows have flown in the brooklet's flood,
And the Showers and Sunshine sport together,
    And the proud Bough boasts of the baby Bud;
On the hillside brown, where the dead leaves linger
    In crackling layers, all crimped and curled,
She parts their folds with a timid finger,
    And shyly peeps at the waking world.

The roystering West Wind flies to greet her,
    And bids her haste, with a gleeful shout:
The quickening Saplings bend to meet her,
    And the first green Grass-blades call, "Come out!"
So, venturing forth with a dainty neatness,
    In gown of pink or in white arrayed,
She comes once more in her fresh completeness,
    A modest, fair little Pilgrim Maid.

Her fragrant petals, their beauties showing,
    Creep out to sprinkle the hill and dell,
Like showers of Stars in the shadows glowing,
    Or Snowflakes blossoming where they fell;
And the charmed Wood leaps into joyous blooming,
    As though 't were touched by a Fairy's ring,
And the glad Earth scents, in the rare perfuming,
    The first sweet breath of the new-born Spring.

Joseph C. Lincoln